Illustrator:
Agi Palinay

Editor:
Stephanie Jona Buehler, M.P.W., M.A.

Editorial Project Manager:
Ina Massler Levin, M.A.

Editor-in-Chief:
Sharon Coan, M.S. Ed.

Art Director:
Elayne Roberts

Associate Designer
Denise Bauer

Cover Artist:
Sue Fullam

Product Manager:
Phil Garcia

Imaging:
David Bennett
Alfred Lau

Publishers:
Rachelle Cracchiolo, M.S. Ed.
Mary Dupuy Smith, M.S. Ed.

Interdisciplinary Unit
Courage
Those Who Dared To Make a Difference
CHALLENGING

Authors:

Cheryl A. Matheson, M.A.
Deborah M. Meres
Linda Smoucha

Teacher Created Materials, Inc.
P.O. Box 1040
Huntington Beach, CA 92647
ISBN-1-55734-620-8

©1996 Teacher Created Materials, Inc.   Made in U.S.A.

Teacher Created Materials

Table of Contents

How to Use This Book 3

What Is Courage? (Teacher Page) 4

What Is Courage? (Student Page) 5

Reading Response Journals 6

The Courage to Resist: *Number the Stars* 7
  (U.S.A.,Dell; Canada; Doubleday Dell Seal; U.K., Lions; Aus., Transworld Pub.)

The Courage to Survive, Part I: *Island of the Blue Dolphins* 45
  (U.S.A., Houghton Mifflin; Canada, Doubleday Dell Seal; U.K., Gollancz Services; Aus., Jackaranda Wiley)

The Courage to Survive, Part II: *Hatchet* 74
  (U.S.A., Penguin; Canada, Penguin; U.K., Pan Books; Aus., Penguin Ltd.)

The Courage to Change Society: *Roll of Thunder, Hear My Cry* 101
  (U.S.A., Canada, U.K., & Aus, Penguin Books)

The Courage to Believe: *Shadow of a Bull* 149
  (U.S.A., Macmillian; Canada, Distican; U.K., Simon & Schuster; Aus., Prentice Hall)

The Courage to Fight: *My Brother Sam Is Dead* 170
  (U.S.A., Scholastic; U.K., Cornerstone; Aus., Ashton Scholastic Party, Ltd.)

Culminating Activities 186

Cover for Response Journal 189

Bibliography 190

Answer Key 193

How to Use This Book

This book emphasizes five different situations in which courage is a necessary quality. "The Courage to Resist" emphasizes the courage it takes to stand up to authority when the authority is operating with questionable conduct. "The Courage to Survive" shows the type of character that is needed to get through a situation by using one's own wits. "The Courage to Change Society" emphasizes that the status quo must sometimes be challenged. "The Courage to Believe" is about faith in one's self and one's dreams and the courage it may take to carry them out. Finally, "The Courage to Fight" is about the bravery demonstrated by soldiers who have gone to war.

These five sections may be taught in the order that best fits your instructional needs. For each section, lessons are planned to extend the theme through a cross-curricular approach. Literature selections provide a foundation for each series of lessons. Some of the pages relate directly to these selections, while others use the selection as a springboard for activities in science, social studies, art, physical education, mathematics, and language arts. It is not necessary to use all of the activities in each section. Use your judgement as to what activities are appropriate for your students. Also consider the amount of time and materials available to you.

As a teacher in a self-contained classroom, you will find activities to meet all your curricular needs. As a content area teacher, you may wish to cooperate with your teaching team and introduce the theme together. Although the lessons in this unit are categorized by content areas, you will find that many of the activities are designed to overlap into more than one curricular area.

What Is Courage?

Neil Armstrong, the first astronaut to walk on the moon, had it. Rosa Parks, the African American woman who refused to relinquish her seat on the bus to a white person in Montgomery, Alabama, had it. The young Chinese man who singlehandedly halted a line of government tanks in Tiananmen Square had it. Today, young people who refuse to submit to peer pressure to join a gang or take drugs most certainly have it.

What is it that these people have in common? In a word, it is courage. Courage is an elusive quality found in the hearts, minds, and spirits of many people. Courage is a quality that knows no racial, religious, or political bounds. Courage comes in many forms, yet it is difficult to define. Webster's *New World Dictionary* speaks of courage as "the attitude of facing and dealing with anything recognized as dangerous, difficult, or painful, instead of withdrawing from it."

While the dictionary definition equates courage with bravery and fearlessness, it is possible to feel afraid and yet still possess courage. The key is not to become immobilized by one's fears, but rather to acknowledge the fear and yet act in spite of it. As Eleanor Roosevelt said in her book, *You Learn by Living,* "You must do the thing you think you cannot do."

Courage can take many forms. For some, courage may mean facing danger on a battlefield. For others, it may mean exploring unknown territories and new frontiers. And for still others, it may mean accepting the daily challenges of growing up in an impoverished neighborhood. Though philosophers, statesmen, writers, and historians throughout the ages have attempted to define courage, it is perhaps best understood in terms of each person's individual life experiences.

We hope this book will help you and your students shape unique definitions of courage which apply to your individual situations and to understand how the courage of a single person can affect an entire society. Throughout this book are thought-provoking activities designed to accomplish these goals. We hope you will share our enthusiasm for this topic, and we wish you much success as you begin to explore the theme of courage.

What Is Courage?

Webster's *New World Dictionary* defines courage as "the attitude of facing and dealing with anything recognized as dangerous, difficult, or painful, instead of withdrawing from it." The pages of history are filled with stories of courageous men and women who fit this definition:

◆ George Washington   ◆ Abraham Lincoln

◆ Neil Armstrong   ◆ Martin Luther King, Jr.

◆ Mother Teresa   ◆ Helen Keller

Completing the following activities will help you to begin thinking about courage and what it means to act courageously.

Activity A: Identify and briefly describe each of the individuals listed above with your class. Why is each individual considered courageous?

Activity B: How each one of you defines courage is shaped by your individual life experiences. With this in mind, consider an individual whom you admire for his or her courage—an historical figure, a well-known public figure, or someone whom you personally know. (It may even be you!) Write a brief description of this person, describing what he or she has done that you feel demonstrates courage.

Activity C: After you have completed Activities A and B, create cooperative learning groups of four to five students. Each member is to read his or her written description to the group. Next, from all those individuals presented, each group must select one person who best illustrates Webster's definition of courage. (**Note to instructor:** You may wish to set a time limit on Activity C.) Once your group has reached a consensus, work together to answer the following questions:

1. Why did your group agree upon this particular individual?

2. Did your group have any difficulty reaching a consensus? Why or why not?

3. What conclusions about courage and individual life experience can you draw from this exercise?

Finally, select a representative from your group to report the results of this activity to your class.

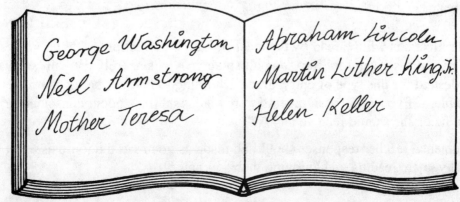

Reading Response Journals

One way to explore literature with your students is to focus on the reader's response. To use this approach, ask your students to keep a journal as they read the novels you will cover. Instruct them to use their journals to record their thoughts, feelings, ideas, and questions which occur to them as they read. These journal entries can then become the basis for class discussions, writing ideas, research topics, and class projects.

This technique encourages students to assume responsibility for their learning. It also allows them to direct the course of what they will learn. Here are a few suggestions for implementing this technique.

- Tell students to record their thoughts, feelings, ideas, and questions as they read each chapter. Emphasize that there is no right or wrong way to respond; they simply are to record whatever they are thinking, feeling, observing, or wondering. Here are a few examples from students' journals, written after reading Chapter 1 of *Number the Stars:*

    — I wonder why Annemarie and Ellen feared the Nazi soldiers, while Kirsti did not.

    — I wonder what it would be like to live without sugar, butter, leather, and electricity.

    — Where is Copenhagen? Why are there German soldiers in the city?

- Ask students to write one new thing that they learned after reading each chapter.

- Have students choose a character in the novel and write their journal entries from that character's point of view.

- Ask students to respond to a particular quotation or to an important passage from the novel.

- Ask students to jot down anything in the novel that arouses their curiosity, such as, What is the Jewish New Year? How does it differ from the national holiday?

- Provide students with, or ask them to suggest, writing topics based upon the novel they are currently reading. Here are some examples of ideas from Chapters 1-3 of *Number the Stars:*

    - Two German soldiers intimidated Annemarie and Ellen as they walked home from school. Think about a time in your life when you felt afraid or when you were intimidated by someone, and then write how you would have felt if German soldiers had stopped you.

    - Annemarie's sister, Lise, was engaged to marry Peter Neilsen; however, she died in an accident two weeks before her wedding. Think about how Annemarie felt about the death of her sister and write about a time in your life when you experienced a loss.

Allow students time to write in their journals daily. To evaluate the journals, you may wish to use the following guidelines.

- Personal reflections will be read by the teacher, but no corrections or letter grades will be assigned. Credit is given for effort, and all students who sincerely try will be awarded credit. If a grade is desired for this type of entry, grade according to the number of journal entries completed. For example, if five journal assignments were made and the student conscientiously completes all five, then he or she should receive an "A."

- Non-judgmental teacher responses should be made as you read the journals to let the students know that you are reading and enjoying their journals.

The Courage to Resist:

Number the Stars

Teacher Information

Previewing the Material

The study of the atrocities against humanity that occurred during the Holocaust may be overwhelming to some students. Before you begin this section, carefully read each activity to decide whether or not it would be appropriate for your students based on their ages and levels of maturity. After determining that an activity is appropriate, allow students both time to complete an activity and time to process their feelings in their journals, in class discussions, and through artwork. Guide students in being supportive of one another's feelings during class discussions.

Begin with the "Introduction to the Holocaust" on page 9 and "Where is Denmark?" on page 10. Then have students read the novel *Number the Stars* and complete the vocabulary and questions that pertain to the novel. It is not intended that you complete all the pages in this section on "The Courage to Resist" nor should you feel obligated to complete all the activities on each page. Use your judgement. Preview each page, always keeping in mind what is appropriate for your individual students as well as the amount of time and materials available for each activity.

Introduction to the Holocaust

During the Holocaust of World War II, six million Jews and five million non-Jews were murdered by the German Nazis under the leadership of Adolph Hitler. Claiming that people of the Jewish race were inferior to people of the Aryan race, Hitler sought to destroy the entire European Jewish population and create a "master race" of Germans. The destruction of a specific race of people is called "genocide," but Hitler and the Nazis used the code name "Final Solution" for their plan, referring to the use of death as an answer to what they perceived as problems created by the existence of Jews.

More than one million children, from infants to teenagers, were killed during the Holocaust. While the majority of victims were Jewish, thousands of Gypsies and Polish Catholics were also executed. Some victims were even murdered because they were mentally or physically handicapped. All of these young victims died because Hitler felt they were inferior to his "master race."

The Nazis sent their victims to killing centers called death camps. Most of these camps were located in Poland, which was occupied by the German army. Here the Nazis gassed their victims, and then burned their bodies in huge furnaces called crematories. They did this to hide the evidence of their crimes from the outside world. Before the victims were murdered, the Nazis stole their belongings. In two death camps alone, Auschwitz-Burkenau and Majdanek, the Nazis stole 300,000 pairs of shoes. (Bachrach, page 102). Crates of wedding rings, mounds of clothing, and tens of thousands of suitcases all served as evidence of Nazi crimes.

It is almost impossible to understand the magnitude of this tragedy. To try to understand the concept of a million children, picture a football stadium like the Rose Bowl in Pasadena, California, which holds approximately 100,000 people. Then, imagine at least ten stadiums like this, all filled with innocent children. Now you have some idea of how many children died in the Holocaust. These children, however, were more than just numbers. Like you, they were individuals with families and friends and lives.

Completing the following activity will help you get a better idea of the size of the number "one million." Try to remember that each unit in the number "one million" represents a human life that was lost.

Activity: In small groups of four to five students, brainstorm ways that you could visually represent the number "one million." Jot down every idea that your group suggests. Then, discuss and choose the idea that would be most practical for your group to do. Complete your project and display it in your classroom or school. With your display, include a brief report about what this number represents.

Where Is Denmark?

Without any prior warning, Germany invaded Denmark on April 9, 1940. Unprepared for this attack, the Danes quickly surrendered. Though Germany officially was not at war with Denmark, German troops occupied this country until the war ended in 1945.

On the nights of October 1 and 2, 1943, the Nazis conducted a secret round-up of Danish Jews for deportation. Approximately 8,000 Jews lived in Denmark at that time, most of them in the capital city of Copenhagen (Petrow, page 204). Three days before the raid occurred, two Danish political leaders were informed of the Nazi's secret plan. These political leaders then told the rabbi in Copenhagen who, in turn, warned his congregation on September 29, the eve of the Jewish New Year. As a result, most Danish Jews were not at home when the Nazi raids took place, and so the arrests number only 284, most of whom were elderly or sick. Over 7,000 Jews survived the raids and eventually escaped to Sweden, which at its closest point is separated from Denmark by only two and one-half miles of water (Petrow, page 227).

Where is Denmark, this small country where people banded together to save a race? Below is a map of Northern Europe. Use an atlas to label the following countries: Denmark, Sweden, Norway, Finland, Holland, Belgium, Switzerland, France, Poland, and Germany. Next, research each of these countries to determine which ones were occupied by the German army during World War II. Then, shade them on the map to complete the assignment.

Summary

Based on factual events, Lois Lowry's novel is set in Denmark during World War II. It is about the compassion and courage of both the Johansen family and a young man named Peter Neilsen (the one-time fiance of the Johansen's deceased daughter, Lise). Together, they rescue their Jewish neighbors, the Rosens, from becoming Holocaust victims. The Johansens have two living daughters: Annemarie, age ten, and Kirsti, age five.

The story begins at the end of September, 1943, significant because it is the time of the Jewish New Year. The German army occupies Denmark and, as an act of persecution, the Nazis have closed down all Jewish businesses. The Rosens' rabbi has told Jewish families that the Nazis will soon raid the homes of Jewish citizens in order to "relocate" them, i.e., send them to concentration camps. To save their lives, the Rosens must be away from home when the Nazis conduct their raid.

The Johansen's offer to hide Ellen Rosen, Annemarie's friend, in their own home by pretending that Ellen is their deceased daughter, Lise. Unfortunately, the Johansen apartment is small, so it is impossible to hide Ellen's parents without the Nazis' knowledge. Mr. and Mrs. Rosen must flee the area altogether in order to survive.

On the night of the raids, the Nazis find the Rosens' apartment empty and decide to search the Johansens' apartment. They suspect that Ellen is Jewish because of her dark hair, but using a clever trick Mr. Johansen deceives the soldiers into believing that Ellen is his deceased daughter, Lise. The Nazi soldiers angrily leave the Johansen apartment.

Still fearing for Ellen's safety, Mrs. Johansen takes Annemarie, Kirsti, and Ellen to the home of her brother, Henrik, a fisherman who lives on the coast of Denmark. With the help of Peter Neilsen, who has been actively involved in the Danish Resistance, Henrik and Mrs. Johansen work together to reunite Ellen with her parents. In an act of daring, Henrik secretly transports the Rosens and other Jewish refugees across the sea to Sweden, which is not occupied by the German army. There the Rosens will remain until the German defeat.

Sadly, during the course of the novel Peter Neilsen is caught by the Nazis and executed for his role in the Danish Resistance; the reader learns that Lise Johansen had been killed by the Nazis for the same reason.

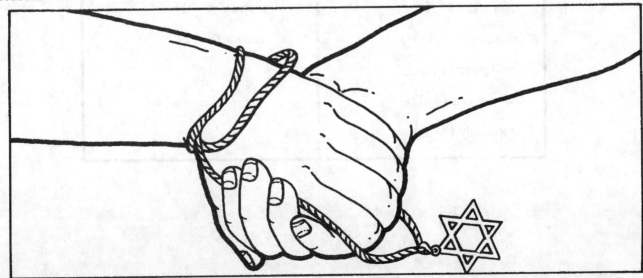

Vocabulary Lists

Below are vocabulary lists which correspond to groups of chapters. Each vocabulary word is followed by two numbers in parentheses; the first number corresponds to the chapter, and the second number corresponds to the page number on which the word may be found. The words are listed in the order in which they appear in the novel. Vocabulary activity ideas can be found on page 14 of this book.

Section 1	**Section 2**
(Chapters 1–4)	(Chapters 5–8)
lanky (1–1)	imperious (5–39)
plodding (1–2)	urgently (5–45)
contempt (1–3)	unwavering (5–48)
prodded (1–3)	clenched (5–49)
obstinate (1–4)	imprinted (5–50)
sabotage (1–8)	tentatively (6–50)
Resistance (1–8)	reluctantly (6–52)
impassive (1–10)	distorted (6–55)
trousseau (2–14)	gnarled (7–60)
intricate (2–14)	ruefully (8–69)
rationed (3–18)	specter (8–69)
swastika (3–21)	dismay (8–71)
exasperated (4–28)	anchor (8–72)
belligerently (4–31)	
submerged (4–32)	
dubiously (4–34)	

Vocabulary Lists (cont.)

Section 3	Section 4	Section 5
(Chapters 9–12)	(Chapters 13–15)	(Chapters 16–17 and Afterword)
deftly (9–75)	faltered (13–101)	hastily (16–120)
hearse (9–77)	donned (14–106)	snarls (16–121)
sulking (9–78)	churning (14–110)	whirled (16–126)
recurring (10–83)	brusque (14–110	complicated (16–126)
staccato (10–83)	prolong (14–112)	shrieked (16–127)
condescending (10–84)	consumed (15–115)	tended (17–128)
typhus (10–85)	withering (15–116)	unoccupied (17–129)
staggered (10–85)	insolently (15–116)	devastating (17–129)
extinguished (10–86)	implored (15–116)	bleak (17–129)
mantel (10–86)	intently (15–116)	bear (17–130)
psalm (10–86)	scornfully (15–116)	clasp (17–132)
binds (10–87)	caustic (15–118)	deprivation (Afterword – 133)
rummaging (11–88)	subsided (15–118)	integrity (Afterword – 133)
encased (11–89)	strident (15–118)	cocaine (Afterword – 136)
protruding (11–91)	din (15–118)	permeated (Afterword – 136)
Godspeed (11–93)	quavering (15–118)	idealistic (Afterword – 136)
Sabbath (11–93)		prejudiced (Afterword – 137)
		decency (Afterword – 137)
		determination (Afterword – 137)

Vocabulary Activities

Here are activities that will help you learn and remember the vocabulary words in *Number the Stars*.

1. Create cooperative learning groups of three to four students and divide the vocabulary words evenly among the group members. For each word received, copy the sentence from the novel in which the word is used, and then write the dictionary definition of the word as it is used in that sentence. When you are finished, share your work with group members so that each person learns the definitions of all the words on the list.

2. With a partner, play vocabulary concentration. You will need two slips of paper for each vocabulary word. Write the word on one slip and the definition on another. Mix up the slips of paper and lay them face down on the desk. Take turns flipping the slips over to see if you can make a match. The person with the most matched pairs at the end of the game is the winner.

3. Hold a vocabulary feud. Form groups of three students, two of whom will be contestants and one of whom will be the "host." First, make a paper buzzer—a red circle in the middle of a piece of white construction paper—and tape it to your desk. Then, the host will state a vocabulary word; the first person to hit the buzzer gives the definition. If that contestant answers incorrectly, the other shall have an opportunity to give the correct definition. Score five points for each correct answer; at the end of the game, the contestant with the most points is the winner.

Questions from the Novel, Chapters 1-4

Directions: After reading Chapters 1-4, answer each of the following questions on the provided lines.

1. What is meant by the term "occupied country?" How did the Nazi occupation of Denmark affect the Johansen family? How did it affect Danish Jews? Find examples from the novel to support your answer.

   _____

   _____

2. Peter Neilsen is a member of the Danish Resistance. Use a dictionary to look up the meaning of the word "resist." How would you define the Danish Resistance? What was their purpose? In what activities were their members involved? Find examples from the novel to support your answer.

   _____

   _____

3. How do the people of Denmark feel about their king, Christian X? Find an example to support your answer.

   _____

   _____

4. What is the purpose of Peter Neilsen's visit to the home of the Johansens? Why is this visit considered dangerous?

   _____

   _____

5. Kirsti speaks of "fireworks" on the night of her birthday late in August. What were these "fireworks" in reality? Why did the Danes do this?

   _____

   _____

6. Why is Ellen staying with the Johansens? Where are Ellen's parents? Why don't they, too, stay with the Johansens?

   _____

   _____

7. How are the Rosens warned in advance of the Nazis' plan to round up the Jews and "relocate" them? _____

   _____

   _____

Questions from the Novel, Chapters 5–8

Directions: After reading Chapters 5–8, answer each of the following questions on the provided lines.

1. What does Annemarie know about Lise's death?

   _____

2. What is the purpose of the Nazis' visit in the middle of the night? How do they treat the Johansen family and Ellen? Find examples to support your answer.

   _____

   _____

3. Why does Annemarie break Ellen's necklace?

   _____

4. What causes the Nazis to suspect that Ellen is Jewish? How does Mr. Johansen deceive the soldiers?

   _____

5. Why do Annemarie's parents prevent Ellen from going to school the next day? Where do the girls and Mrs. Johansen go instead? Why doesn't Mr. Johansen accompany them?

   _____

   _____

6. Mr. Johansen speaks in code when he telephones Henrik. Describe this conversation, and then explain what Mr. Johansen really means.

   _____

7. Why does a German soldier aboard the train ask Mrs. Johansen if she is going to visit her brother for the New Year?

   _____

8. What does Annemarie fear Kirsti will say? Do you think Mr. and Mrs. Johansen should have told Kirsti about their plan? Explain why or why not.

   _____

   _____

9. What has Annemarie done with Ellen's necklace?

   _____

10. Why does Annemarie suspect that Great-Aunt Birte does not exist?

   _____

Questions from the Novel, Chapters 9–12

Directions: After reading Chapters 9–12, answer each of the following questions on the provided lines.

1. Annemarie wonders if she should tell Ellen the truth about Great-Aunt Birte. Why does Annemarie decide to say nothing?

   _____

2. Who are the people who come to Henrik's house? Compare and contrast the wake held for Great-Aunt Birte and the wake held for Lise.

   _____

   _____

3. In Chapter 10, Annemarie hears "the pounding on the door, and then the heavy, frightening familiar staccato of boots on the kitchen floor." Define "staccato," and then tell what is happening in this scene. Next look up the meaning of the word "recur," then tell why Annemarie refers to this scene as "a recurring nightmare."

   _____

   _____

4. What causes the Nazi soldiers to be suspicious about this wake?

   _____

5. Define "typhus," and then tell how Mrs. Johansen uses it to deceive the Nazi soldiers.

   _____

   _____

6. What is the purpose of Peter's visit to the home of Henrik?

   _____

7. What is in the casket when Peter opens it? Why are these things needed?

   _____

8. What does Peter give the baby Rachel? Why does he do this? Do you think this is necessary? Explain your answer.

   _____

9. What does Peter ask Mr. Rosen to do as they leave Henrik's house? Explain this scene.

   _____

10. In your own words, tell what Peter instructs Mrs. Johansen to do.

    _____

11. How has Peter changed from the boy who once courted Lise?

    _____

12. When Annemarie awakens, what time is it? Where is her mother?

    _____

    _____

    _____

    _____

Questions from the Novel, Chapters 13–15

Directions: After reading Chapters 13–15, answer each of the following questions on the provided lines.

1. What happens to Mrs. Johansen on the path leading from the harbor to Henrik's house?

    _____

2. Why do you think Henrik waited until dawn to leave the harbor in his boat?

    _____

3. Annemarie finds the packet that Peter gave to Mr. Rosen near Henrik's house. What does Annemarie volunteer to do? How does her mother help Annemarie disguise the true purpose of her mission?

    _____

    _____

4. Why does Annemarie think it is safer to stay on the path through the woods rather than take the road to the harbor?

    _____

5. Why do you think Annemarie recalls the story of "Little Red Riding Hood" as she hurries toward the harbor?

    _____

6. What happens to Annemarie on the way to the harbor?

    _____

7. How does Annemarie explain to the Nazis her purpose for travelling to the harbor so early?

    _____

8. Find an example of how Annemarie acts like her younger sister, Kirsti, in the woods. Why does she do this? Does it work? Explain your answer.

    _____

    _____

9. Do you think that it is easier for Annemarie to be brave because she didn't know what was in the packet? Explain your answer.

    _____

10. What happens when Annemarie reaches the harbor?

    _____

    _____

Questions from the Novel, Chapters 16–17 and Afterword

Directions: After reading Chapters 16–17 and the Afterword, answer each of the following questions on the provided lines.

1. What does Mrs. Johansen tell Kirsti about Ellen the next morning?

   _____

   _____

2. What does Henrik tell Annemarie when they go to the barn together to milk the cow?

   _____

3. Why do the Germans use dogs to search the boats in the harbor?

   _____

   _____

4. What is in the handkerchief that Annemarie brings to Henrik? What effect does it have on the dogs?

   _____

5. What is Peter's role in the escapes?

   _____

   _____

6. How do the people of Denmark celebrate the end of World War II in May of 1945? How do they prepare for the return of their Jewish friends and neighbors?

   _____

   _____

7. What happens to Peter Neilsen? How do you feel about this?

   _____

8. Explain the truth about Lise's death.

   _____

   _____

9. Where has Annemarie hidden Ellen's necklace? What does Annemarie plan to do with the necklace?

   _____

10. Work with a partner to complete the following. After rereading the "Afterword" of *Number the Stars*, divide a sheet of paper into two columns. Label one column "fiction" and the other "non-fiction." In the appropriate columns, list the story events that are true and the story events that are fiction.

    _____

Thinking About the Novel

In Chapter 10 of *Number the Stars*, Peter Neilsen reads a passage from the Bible at the wake of Great-aunt Birte. This passage, shown below, refers to a time centuries ago when Jews also were in exile.

O praise the Lord.
How good it is to sing psalms to our God!
How pleasant to praise Him!
The Lord is rebuilding Jerusalem
to gather in the scattered sons of Israel.
It is He who heals the broken in spirit
and binds up their wounds,
He who numbers the stars one by one.

The passage concerns a promise God made to the prophet Abraham that his descendants would be as plentiful as the stars in the sky. How does this idea relate to the title of the novel you have just read? Completing the following activities will help you understand the meaning of the title. Refer to the Bible passage as needed.

Activity A: Answer the following questions:

1. Think about the people gathered at the wake of Great-aunt Birte. Who are these people? Where are they about to go?

   _____

2. Why might Peter have chosen to read this particular passage at the wake of Great-aunt Birte?

   _____

3. How does Annemarie feel as she listens to Peter read these words from the Bible? What is she thinking?

   _____

4. Think about the novel's title. What do you think it means?

   _____

Activity B: Creatively apply what you have learned about the novel by choosing one of these art projects.

Imagine that you have been chosen to illustrate the cover of *Number the Stars*. Create a cover using whatever materials are available to you. Display the covers in either the classroom or school.

Working in small groups or as a class, paint a mural of stars shining brightly in the night sky. Display the mural in either your classroom or school.

The Swastika

In the novel *Number the Stars*, Annemarie, Ellen, and Kirsti visit Mrs. Hirsch's button shop, but when they arrive the shop is locked and there is a sign on the door in German. The girls walk home and tell Mrs. Johansen what they have seen. Worried by this news, Mrs. Johansen asks, "Are you sure the sign was in German?"

"Mama, it had a swastika on it," Annemarie replies.

The swastika is the symbol for the Nazi party. Nazi leader Adolph Hitler wanted a banner and symbol behind which the German people could rally. The black swastika in a stark circle of white centered on a red banner became that symbol, representing in essence the anti-Jewish sentiments of the Nazi party.

The swastika consists of a cross with its four "arms" bent at a 90° angle in a clockwise direction. The swastika itself seems to rotate, reflecting the notion that the German army was on the move. Hitler understood the power of this symbol and became obsessed by it, worshipping it with almost a religious enthusiasm. He wanted other Germans to share his fervor; after he became chancellor of Germany in 1933, the Nazi party passed a law banning all political symbols except the swastika (*Liungman*, pages 66–67).

Since Hitler's ultimate goal was to wipe out the entire Jewish race, he referred to his plan as the "Final Solution." Under his leadership, the Nazis murdered six million Jews in Europe between 1933 and 1945—two-thirds of the total population of European Jews. The Nazis also murdered millions of other innocent non-Jews whom they considered to be inferior or enemies of Germany.

Because the swastika was associated with Nazi atrocities, it has come to represent the evil within human nature and has become, perhaps, one of the most hated symbols in history. After Hitler and Germany lost the war in 1945, the swastika was banned from public display.

The following activity will acquaint you with the concept of symbols and help you understand the effect symbols can have upon us.

Activity: Create cooperative learning groups of four to five students. Then imagine that you are members of the Danish resistance and create a symbol for your movement. (You may wish to refer to a dictionary of symbols or signs; check your library to see if this type of reference is available.) Discuss your ideas, sketching them on paper. Try to make your group's symbol as powerful as the swastika you are opposing. Each group then will decide which of the proposed symbols it likes best and display it on a banner. The banners can then be displayed in either your classroom or school.

The Star of David

A symbol of Judaism, the Star of David is created by two triangles that interlock to form a six-pointed star. During the Middle Ages (500-1450 A.D.), Jews displayed this six-pointed star on their banners and prayer shawls to identify themselves. But during World War II, the Nazis used the six-pointed star to identify the Jews for evil purposes. In almost every country occupied by Germans, Jews age six and older were required to wear a yellow Star of David either sewn or pinned to their outer garment or on an arm band.

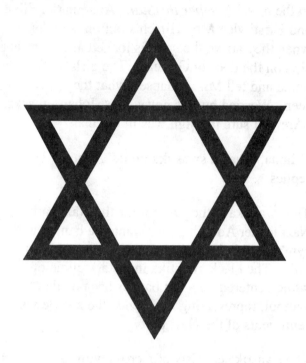

When the Nazis invaded Denmark, however, Danish Jews were not required to wear this symbol on their clothing because the Danish government insisted that Danish Jews were citizens just like all other Danes and were not to be discriminated against. In fact, Danish Jews in occupied Denmark were able to live in relative freedom until 1943.

Complete one or more of the following activities to help you become more aware of how the Star of David symbol is used in the Jewish religion and culture.

Activity A: The Star of David currently appears on the flag of Israel. Work with a partner to research this flag and make a replica using whatever materials are available to you. Display the flag in your classroom.

Activity B: Make a bookmark that includes the Star of David symbol.

Activity C: Work in small groups to research the name of a Jewish newspaper. Find out if the newspaper displays the Star of David. If possible, obtain and bring a copy of the newspaper to class. What kinds of articles and advertising does the newspaper contain? Does the newspaper include an editorial section where the readers and the editors can express their opinions on different subjects? Cut out several articles or editorials to discuss with your classmates, and display them in your classroom.

Activity D: Research the name of a Jewish organization and obtain written information, such as a pamphlet, to learn more about it. You might also invite a member of the organization to speak to your class about the purpose of the organization and the work the members do. Remember to prepare a list of questions in advance for your speaker.

Activity E: As a class project, you might visit a synagogue together and arrange for a rabbi to speak to your class about Jewish traditions or the Holocaust. Notice what, if any, symbols are found within the synagogue itself.

The Danish Resistance

Germany began its occupation of Denmark in 1940. Unlike the Jews in other German-occupied countries of Europe, Danish Jews were allowed to live in relative freedom. In fact, from 1940 to 1943, Danish Jews were permitted to own property and operate businesses, they were not herded into ghettos and starved as were other European Jews. Danish Jews were not required to wear a yellow Star of David on their clothing nor were they rounded up and deported to death camps.

On September 28, 1943, everything changed when a German official in Copenhagen, George Duckwitz, informed two Danish political leaders of a secret Nazi plan to raid and deport Danish Jews. The political leaders then told the rabbi in Copenhagen what they had learned. At first, this Jewish religious leader did not believe the raids would take place. He waited a day before warning his congregation of the Nazi plan until on September 29—the eve of the Jewish New Year. The bad news rapidly spread by word of mouth throughout the Jewish community.

The people of Denmark reacted with anger. Just two days before the Nazi raids, the Danes managed to hide their fellow Jewish citizens until escape plans could be made. Danes not only hid friends but also sheltered total strangers and often gave them money as well.

Danish bishops protested the deportation of Jews and urged their congregations not to cooperate with the Germans. Members of the medical profession disguised Jews as patients and hid them in hospitals. Fishermen used their boats to transport Jews to Sweden. Even the Danish police, who were supposed to enforce Nazi laws, helped Jewish refugees escape by sea. Of all the occupied countries in Europe during World War II, only Denmark managed to save most of its Jewish population.

The following activity will help you imagine what it was like to be a member of the courageous Danish resistance movement.

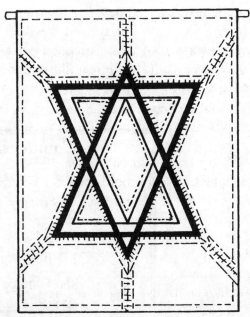

Activity: Imagine that you are a Resistance fighter, as well as a writer for the illegal newspaper, *DeFrie Danske* ("The Free Danes"). Create cooperative learning groups of four to five students to publish your own issue of this newspaper. You will probably need to do research before you begin. A good place to look is in books about the Holocaust, checking their table of contents and index pages to see if they contain information about the Danish resistance. *Rescue: The Story of How Gentiles Saved Jews in the Holocaust* by Milton Meltzer (Harper & Row, 1988) is an excellent resource.

Another approach to this assignment is to write your own newspaper-type stories about the Danish Resistance based on information you read in *Number the Stars*. On the front page of your newspaper, use the symbol you have created for the Danish Resistance from page 21 of this book. You may also wish to publish your newspaper on a computer if one is available to you, although you must remember computers and telecommunications equipment were not available during World War II.

Others Who Resisted

The people of Denmark were not the only Europeans who resisted Nazi persecution of Jews. Thousands of Jews were saved by people in other countries as well. For instance, Belgians rescued 29,000 Jews—more than half the Jewish population living in Belgium between 1940 and 1941. (Meltzer, page 141)

Complete one or both of the following activities to help you discover what other courageous people did to help save Jewish lives during the Holocaust.

Activity A: A fascinating book about Holocaust survivors has been written by Maxine B. Rosenberg, entitled *Hiding to Survive*. The book contains first-person accounts of fourteen adults who recall their experiences as children in hiding during the Nazi regime. Select one of the stories and write a summary about what you have learned. Include a paragraph or two in which you personally respond to the story you chose, telling what you thought and felt as you read the individual's account.

Activity B: Create cooperative learning groups of 3-4 students to investigate either one of the countries or the people listed below and write a report. If you choose a country, write a report on how Gentiles (non-Jews) there courageously resisted the Nazi persecution of the Jews. Include a map of the country with your report. If you choose a person, include a map of the country this person was from. Also include one or two original illustrations in your report. Then share this information with your classmates.

Countries	People
Belgium	Oskar Schindler (Poland)
Germany	Andre Trocmé (Le Chambon, France)
Holland	
Italy	Raoul Wallenberg (Hungary)
the Ukraine	

The Purpose and Use of Passports

As you read about the Holocaust, you may find yourself wondering why the Jews did not simply flee Germany to escape the Nazis. But remember, Germany invaded and occupied many of the countries in Europe during World War II. Often there was no place for the Jews to go.

In order to leave a country in which you have citizenship, you need to have official documents, such as a passport. Then, even if you hold the required documents to enter another country legally, the other country must be willing to accept you. The voyage of the *S.S. St. Louis*, a German steamship, illustrates the terrible situation in which Jews often found themselves. In 1939, 936 passengers aboard the *S.S. St. Louis*, almost all of whom were Jewish, sailed from Germany to Cuba to escape the Nazis. When their ship arrived in Havana, these passengers were not allowed to enter the country. Even though they held the proper visas (official permission documents), the Cuban government refused them entry.

The *S.S. St. Louis* then left Cuba, and the ship's captain requested permission from the American government to allow the passengers to enter the United States. Permission was denied, and the ship returned to Europe, where passengers were accepted by England, France, Holland, and Belgium. The passengers who emigrated to England were safe, but most of those accepted by the other three countries were killed once those countries were invaded by Nazis. (Bachrach, page 28)

A passport allows U.S. citizens to travel outside the United States. It also contains a request that foreign governments protect and aid the bearer of the U.S. passport. Here is a sample passport for a U.S. citizen. Read it carefully.

United States of America Passport Number

(photograph)

Surname_____
(last name)

Given names _____
(first and middle names)

Nationality_____

Date of birth_____

Sex_____

Place of birth_____

Date of issue_____

Date of expiration_____

Authority_____
(where the passport was issued)

Signature of bearer_____

(page 1)

Bearer's address in the United States
_____
_____
_____

Bearer's foreign address
_____
_____
_____

In case of accident or death, notify the nearest American embassy and the person listed below.

Name_____

Address
_____
_____

Telephone_____

(page 2)

Making a Passport

Fill in the blanks below as if it were your passport. Glue a small photograph of yourself in the space provided. Cut out your passport and make a cover and endsheets so that it looks like a small booklet. Perhaps you could make an official-looking stamp for the front cover of your document.

United States of America
Passport Number

(photograph)

Surname _____
(*last name*)

Given names _____
(*first and middle names*)

Nationality_____

Date of birth _____

Sex_____

Place of birth_____

Date of issue _____

Date of expiration _____

Authority _____
(*where the passport was issued*)

Signature of bearer _____

Bearer's address in the United States

_____

_____

_____

Bearer's foreign address

_____

_____

_____

In case of accident or death, notify the nearest American embassy and the person listed below.

Name _____

Address

_____

_____

Telephone _____

Why Remember the Holocaust?

The idea of creating The United States Holocaust Memorial Museum in Washington, D.C. was controversial even before it was built. Some people wanted to know why such a museum was being built in the United States rather than in Germany where the Holocaust occurred. Other people felt that Americans first needed to honor the African-American struggle for equal rights. Some argued that Americans needed to recognize the persecution of Native American Indians during the early history of our country. Still others believed it was best to just forget about the Holocaust; since it happened over 50 years ago, why dig up the past? ("We Are Witnesses," page 48).

In 1993, the American Jewish Committee published the results of a survey about the Holocaust that questioned a cross section of people throughout the United States. A "cross section" means many types of people—men and women, blacks and whites, wealthy and poor, students and adults, educated and uneducated—were surveyed. The survey results were surprising. Twenty-eight percent of those surveyed did not know anything about the Holocaust. Twenty percent of the people who had heard about the Holocaust believed it was possible that the Holocaust never happened; in other words, they could deny that the Holocaust ever occurred. It is partly in response to people's lack of information and denial that Holocaust museums exist today ("Yes and No," page 29).

During World War II, Dwight D. Eisenhower was the commanding general of American troops in Europe; later, he became the 34th President of the United States. At the end of World War II, General Eisenhower entered one of the Nazi death camps where thousands of Jews were murdered. In the following quotation, General Eisenhower responds to what he witnessed and explains why he personally visited one of the Nazi death camps:

> *The things I saw beggar description. . . The visual evidence and the verbal testimony of starvation, cruelty, and bestiality were so overpowering. . . I made the visit deliberately, in order to be in a position to give firsthand evidence of these things if ever, in the future, there develops a tendency to charge these allegations to propaganda.*

General Eisenhower's words are carved into the wall at the entrance of the United States Holocaust Memorial Museum in Washington, D.C.

Work in small groups of four to five students to complete the following activities. They will help you understand why it is important to remember the Holocaust.

Activity A: To better understand General Eisenhower's quotation, use a dictionary to look up the meanings of the words "allegation" and "propaganda." Discuss what these words mean within the context of the quotation, and then write what you think General Eisenhower meant by his words.

Activity B: Conduct a survey on the Holocaust. As a class question a total of 100 people. Strive for a cross-section of respondents. Be sure to ask if they have ever heard of the Holocaust and if they believe that it happened. Make a chart or graph to display your results. How do the results of your survey compare with those of the American Jewish Committee?

Holocaust Museums and Information Organizations

In Israel today exists a special place, a research center on the Holocaust called Yad Vashem. The center includes a museum, a library, and archives (historical records) about the Holocaust. In this place are recorded not only atrocities, but also the good deeds of Gentiles who helped Jews during the Holocaust.

Choose one of the following activities to help you learn more about Yad Vashem and other Holocaust museums and organizations.

Activity A: Create cooperative learning groups of three to four students to find out more about Yad Vashem, including what kinds of materials are stored there. As you do your research, find out about the Avenue of the Righteous, which leads to Yad Vashem's Holocaust Museum. Write a brief report that includes significant details about Yad Vashem and perhaps an illustration of the Avenue of the Righteous. Then, share what your group has learned with your class.

Activity B: Besides Yad Vashem in Israel, there are several Holocaust museums and organizations located in the United States. The United States Holocaust Memorial Museum in Washington, D.C., is one of the most recent of such museums to open. This museum commissioned a book specifically designed for middle school students to learn about the Holocaust: *Tell Them We Remember: The Story of the Holocaust* by Susan D. Bachrach (Little, Brown, & Company: Boston, 1994). The book may be available in your school or public library and would be a good resource for this activity. Create cooperative learning groups of three to four students and choose a Holocaust museum or organization from the list below that you would like to know more about. Call or write to your chosen institution to obtain magazine and newspaper article reprints, copies of its newsletter, or brochures which it publishes. Then write a brief report based on what your group has learned. Illustrate your report with either original artwork or photographs from brochures or newsletters that you may receive. Share what you have learned with your class.

(Note for instructor: Some Holocaust museums contain very graphic photographs depicting the horror of the Holocaust; for that reason, field trips are not advisable as the content may be overwhelming for middle school students.)

Facing History and Ourselves National Foundation
25 Kennard Road
Brookline, MA 02146
(617)232-1595

Holocaust Memorial Foundation of Illinois
4255 Main Street
Skokie, IL 60076
(708)677-4640

Simon Wiesenthal Center
9760 W. Pico Blvd.
Los Angeles, CA 90035
(213)490-2525

United States Holocaust Memorial Museum
100 Raoul Wallenberg Place, S.W.
Washington, D.C. 20024-2150
(202)488-0400

Personal Response to the Holocaust

The United States Holocaust Memorial Museum is located in Washington, D.C. Opened in 1993, the museum is dedicated to the memory of the millions of people murdered by the Nazis between 1933 and 1945. The museum's purpose is to help the living remember those killed in the Holocaust with the hope that such genocide never again will be repeated.

The museum contains many artifacts from World War II. There are suitcases that Jews carried to the concentration camps and the identification badges that Jews were made to wear. Two of the largest artifacts found in the museum are a railroad freight car like those used to transport Jews to death camps in Poland and a small Danish boat that was used by members of the Danish resistance to transport Jews to freedom in Sweden. The museum also holds photographs of Jewish prisoners and oral histories of survivors.

The museum also has a unique mural entitled the Wall of Remembrance. The mural contains more than 3,000 tiles created by American children who learned about the Holocaust. The tiles are an expression of how these children felt about those who were murdered by the Nazis.

The following activity will give you the opportunity to personally express your own feelings about the Holocaust.

Activity: As a class project, make your own Wall of Remembrance for those who died in the Holocaust. Create cooperative learning groups of four to five students to discuss your ideas. Would you like to paint square tiles like the ones displayed in the United States Holocaust Memorial Museum? Would you like to make a quilt with each person contributing one square to the overall design? What other ideas do you have?

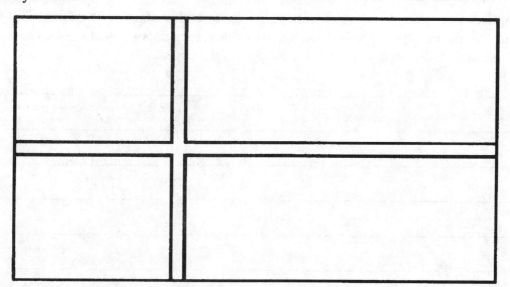

Something else for your group to consider is where you will display your Wall of Remembrance, as this may influence the type of project your class will choose to complete. You may also wish to discuss whether you will use words, artwork, or both to express your feelings.

When you have finished your discussion, choose a representative to share your group's ideas with the class. Then have a class vote on which of the projects you will complete.

Additional Research Questions

Choose one of the following questions as a starting point for learning more about the Holocaust. Research information in books, magazines, newspapers, and encyclopedias, using at least three resources. Write a brief, illustrated report on what you have learned that includes facts, details, and specific examples. You may include maps and photographs along with hand drawn pictures. Be sure that your report also explains how the question you have researched pertains to the Holocaust. When you have finished, orally present your written report to your class.

- What were the Nuremberg Trials in Germany in 1945 and 1946?

- Who was Adolph Eichmann?

- Who was Simon Wiesenthal?

- What happened to Danish Jews when they returned to Denmark after World War II?

- What role did the United States play during the Holocaust? Was the United States willing to take in Jewish immigrants?

- What was the Warsaw Ghetto Uprising?

- What was life like in the Jewish ghettos?

- What was the Evian Conference held in 1938?

- What was Kristallnacht or "The Night of Broken Glass"?

- How was Sweden able to remain neutral during World War II?

Another option is to create cooperative learning groups to brainstorm your own questions about the Holocaust. Use the lines below to list your questions, and then choose one to research. Again, when you have finished, orally present your group's report to the class.

_____

_____

_____

_____

_____

_____

_____

_____

_____

Debating an Issue

A debate is a discussion or argument on a controversial topic. The topic to be debated is usually known as the question. The debate question should be something that can be argued both for and against and is always stated in the affirmative (in favor). For instance, a debate might begin with the following proposition: "Holocaust museums serve a useful purpose."

During the debate, one team argues for and one team argues against the question. In the opening speech, each team in turn tries to persuade the audience or judge to agree with them, using facts to support their position. In the portion of the debate known as the rebuttal, each team tries to point out errors in the opponents' thinking. Note: Sometimes in a debate you must argue for a side that goes against your opinion.

Activity: In preparation for a debate, work in groups of eight students to brainstorm a list of ideas for topics about the Holocaust, remembering that topics for a debate must be controversial. Then, vote on the topic you would like to debate, with four students arguing for the question and four students arguing against the question. You may not necessarily agree with the position that you are defending. Be sure each team has an equal amount of time to speak. Here is a short format you may wish to follow for your debate:

Opening speech in favor *(5-10 minutes)*

Opening speech against *(5-10 minutes)*

Rebuttal speech in favor *(3-5 minutes)*

Rebuttal speech against *(3-5 minutes)*

The key to a successful debate is preparation. Before you debate a topic, thoroughly research it by reading newspaper and magazine articles, books, etc. Take notes on the issues which may be debated, and then discuss these issues with the members of your debate team. Once you have decided what the important issues are, look for the strongest evidence you can find to support your position.

Debating an Issue *(cont.)*

You should also take notes on facts, reasons, examples, statistics, and other evidence that will support your position. Avoid using emotions to prove your argument. You should also avoid using your own opinion, but direct quotes from experts can be used to strengthen your position.

Next, prepare the opening speech and an outline of a rebuttal to what you believe will be your opposing team's arguments. During the actual debate, listen carefully and take notes as the opposing team speaks. Do the opposing team's arguments make sense? Are their arguments based on fact, opinion, or emotion? Do their conclusions fit the evidence you found in researching the topic? Use this information to prepare your rebuttal.

Ask for a volunteer to moderate the debate. As a class, discuss what responsibilities the moderator will have. You might also make a poster advertising your debate so that other classes may come to listen.

Note: *How to Debate* by Robert E. Dunbar (Franklin Watts: New York, 1994) is a good resource for more detailed information.

Poetry: "The Courage That My Mother Had"

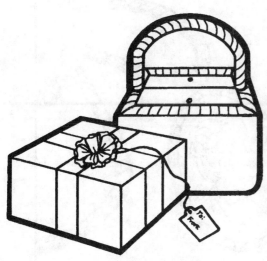

Annemarie demonstrated courage throughout *Number the Stars,* especially when she went alone to deliver the secret packet to Henrik. How did she learn to be so courageous? Perhaps it is because Annemarie's parents were excellent role models. Both parents faced great danger when they hid Ellen from the Nazis, and Mrs. Johansen bravely handled the Nazis' questions at Great-aunt Birte's funeral. These acts of courage were special gifts Annemarie received from her family.

Think about a gift that you have received. Why did that gift mean so much to you? Perhaps it was valuable in monetary terms, or perhaps it was something for which you had wished. Perhaps it was meaningful or sentimental because someone special had given it to you.

Edna St. Vincent Millay (1892-1950), a well-known American poet, expressed her feelings about the best gift she ever received in the poem, "The Courage That My Mother Had."

"The Courage That My Mother Had"
The courage that my mother had
Went with her, and is with her still:
Rock from New England quarried:
Now granite in a granite hill.

The golden brooch my mother wore
She left behind for me to wear:
I have no thing I treasure more:
Yet, it is something I could spare:
Oh, if instead she'd left to me
The thing she took into the grave!

That courage like a rock, which she
Has no more need of, and I have.

Complete one or more of the following activities to help you better understand the meaning of St. Vincent Millay's poem.

Activity A: Write the answers to the following questions. Discuss as a class.

1. In the first stanza, the speaker compares her mother to a rock. Why is a rock a good choice?
2. What does the speaker inherit from her mother? How does she feel about this object?
3. What does the speaker mean by the line, "Yet, it is something I could spare"?
4. What does the speaker wish she had inherited from her mother? Why?
5. Can a parent pass down a quality to a child? Explain your answer.

Poetry: "The Courage That My Mother Had" *(cont.)*

Activity B: In the poem, "The Courage That My Mother Had," Edna St. Vincent Millay refers to the "golden brooch my mother wore." When such a valuable item is willed to an individual, it is referred to as an "heirloom." Do you have any family heirlooms? If so, what are they? What special meaning or significance do they hold for your family? If you were to pass down an heirloom to your future generations, what would it be? Why did you select this particular thing? What does it say about you? For example, do you value your stamp or baseball card collection? Write a brief essay expressing your ideas.

Activity C: Make a list of what you believe to be your five best qualities.

1. _____

2. _____

3. _____

4. _____

5. _____

Once you have completed your list, team up with a person in your class who knows you well. Have your partner list what he or she believes are your five best qualities. Then compare the lists.

1. _____

2. _____

3. _____

4. _____

5. _____

Are any of the qualities the same? Do you think of these qualities as family traits? If so, identify the family member from whom you inherited these qualities. Share your thoughts with your class.

Activity D: In the poem "The Courage That My Mother Had," the speaker wishes she had inherited her mother's courage. What special quality would you like to inherit from one or both of your parents? You might, for example, select your mother's patience or your father's sense of humor. Share your thoughts with your class.

Anne Frank: The Diary of a Young Girl

Anne Frank was a Jewish girl born in Frankfurt, Germany, in 1929. Her family lived in Germany until 1933, the year that Adolph Hitler rose to power and the Nazis began to persecute Jews. To escape anti-Semitism, Anne's family moved to Holland where, for a while, they were able to live normal lives.

In 1940, however, Nazi German soldiers invaded Holland and placed many restrictions upon the Jews. Jews were forced to wear yellow Stars of David and were made to attend segregated Jewish schools. They had an eight o'clock curfew and so could not attend theaters, concerts, or museums. They also were forbidden from operating businesses and practicing their professions.

In early 1941, Nazis attacked Jews on the streets of Amsterdam and burned their synagogues. Although both Jews and Christians resisted, the Nazis overpowered them and sent 425 Jews to their death at Mauthausen Camp. The Nazis also arrested non-Jewish workers who went on strike to protest the persecution of Jews.

Then, on July 5, 1942, Anne Frank's sixteen year old sister, Margot, was summoned for deportation. The Frank family made a decision to go into hiding in the secret annex of an old office building prepared by Anne's father and some of his Christian friends. The Franks were joined in the annex by Mr. and Mrs. Van Dan, their son Peter, and Mr. Dussel, a dentist. Anne Frank was 13 years old at the time.

Anne Frank: The Diary of a Young Girl *(cont.)*

The Frank family remained hidden for about two years until they were betrayed and discovered in August 1944. Of the eight people taken from the annex by the Nazis, only Anne's father, Otto, survived the Holocaust; Anne died in a concentration camp just a few months before the war ended. While in hiding, Anne recorded her thoughts and feelings in a diary that she never intended to share with anyone. But Otto Frank found the diary in the annex after Anne's arrest and had it published after the war in honor of his family. Although Anne died in the Holocaust, her voice, preserved in the pages of one of the most-read books in the world, can still be heard today.

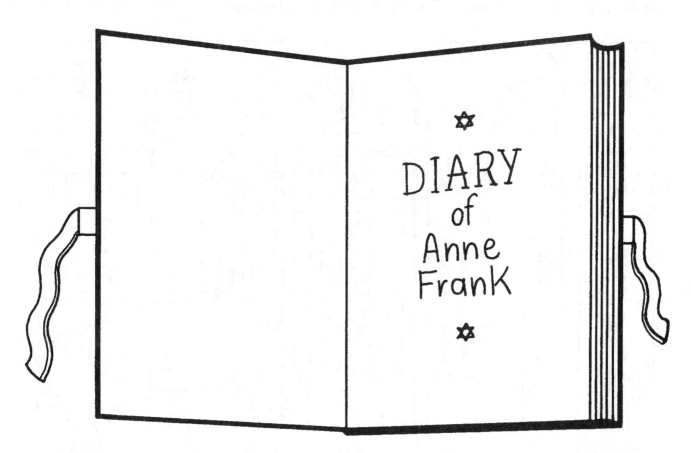

Complete one or more of the following activities to help you learn more about Anne Frank and her feelings about the Holocaust. The activities will also give you the opportunity to express your own feelings about the Holocaust or other subjects.

Activity A: Create cooperative learning groups of three to four students. Have each group member select and write a brief summary of five excerpts from *Anne Frank: The Diary of a Young Girl*, and then share what they have written with the group.

Activity B: Write a brief entry in your reading response journal, responding personally to what you have read in Anne's diary.

Activity C: Keep a personal diary for one month. Record the events of your daily life, as well as your innermost thoughts and feelings. You need not share this diary with anyone. At the end of the month, read to yourself what you have written. You may find that you wish to continue writing in a diary.

Writing a Letter

Choose one of the following letter-writing activities in order to respond emotionally to what you have learned about the Holocaust. Jot down your ideas, then write your actual letter on separate paper. Be sure to date the letter to reflect the historical period in which you are writing. When you and your classmates have completed these activities, you may wish to collect the letters into a booklet or otherwise display them in your classroom or school.

Activity A: Imagine that you are the character of Ellen Rosen and that you and your family have just escaped to Sweden. At this point you do not know if you will ever be able to return to Denmark again.

Write a letter to Annemarie explaining how you feel about what has happened to you and your family. Think about what emotions you might be experiencing. In your letter, tell Annemarie how you feel about her family as well. At the end of your letter, explain to Annemarie why you have decided not to mail this letter. Instead, what will you do with it?

Activity B: Imagine that you are a young Jewish person who has been forcibly taken from your home by the Nazis. You are now living in a Nazi concentration camp. Imagine that you could somehow get a letter to the outside world to someone who might rescue you. Then write to him or her. Think about the feelings you are experiencing. What would you say in your letter?

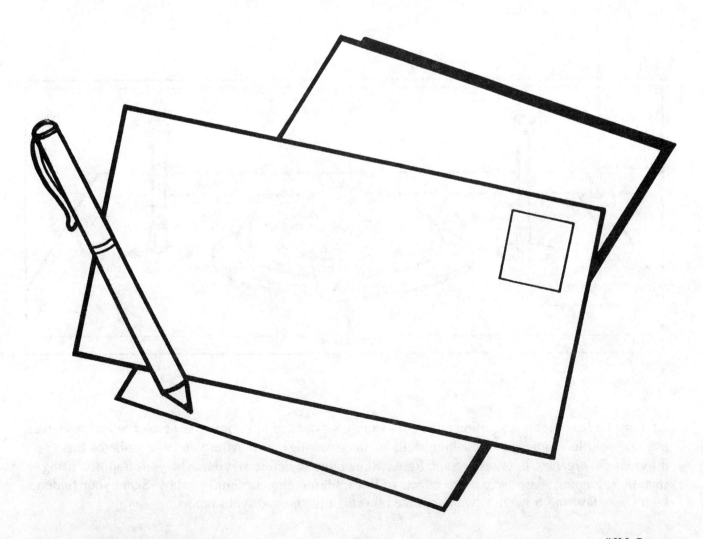

Traditions: A Family Affair

What is tradition? According to Webster's dictionary, tradition is defined as a "long established custom or practice that has been handed down orally from one generation to another." Traditions can be thought of as links that provide us with an awareness of our roots. Every country and culture has its own unique customs and traditions. Choose one of the following activities to help you understand the meaning of tradition.

Activity A: In the novel *Number the Stars*, Lois Lowry refers to several Jewish traditions, including Rosh Hashanah (the celebration of the new year) and the lighting of the candles at sundown on the Sabbath. Looking back through the novel, recall how the Rosens observed or celebrated these occasions. Research and write an illustrated report about one of these traditions. If you are Jewish, write a narrative based on your personal experience with these traditions and bring to class any associated objects.

Activity B: Here are some other Jewish traditions: keeping a kosher home, breaking a glass during a wedding ceremony, disallowing marriages on the Sabbath, women covering their heads at all times. (Note: There are different branches of Judaism, with some branches following ancient laws more closely than others.) Choose one of the traditions listed and find out its religious significance. How is it an important part of Jewish family life? If you are Jewish, you may discuss a Jewish tradition based upon your own experience.

Activity C: Investigate a tradition or custom from your own culture. Relatives are excellent resources; practice your listening and note-taking skills by interviewing them. After you have gathered this information, organize it into paragraph form. Remember to define and describe your tradition using specific examples. Also include the effects of this tradition on your family today. Share your findings with your class and bring in any appropriate objects or pictures for your report.

Traditional Dance

Another part of many people's traditional backgrounds is the art of dance. Dancing is considered a very early form of communication. Today, dances are performed on special occasions and are an important component of some religious practices. Some traditional dances with which you may be familiar are the hora, polka, and the Irish jig.

Complete one or both of the following activities to help you learn more about traditional dance.

Activity A, Part I: Either by speaking to relatives or using reference materials for information, explore your own culture by investigating a traditional folk dance. Include the origin of the dance and a brief description of the basic steps.

Activity A, Part II: Now that you have discovered your own folk dance tradition, be prepared to teach it to someone else. Bring in any music or props that would be appropriate for your lesson. Some examples are traditional clothing (Indian headdress, sombrero) or a musical instrument (accordion, castanets).

Activity B: Research the origin of the following dances: flamenco, hora, polka, tango, ballet, waltz, Cossack. Briefly describe each dance and its origins.

Traditional Clothing

The way a person dresses is a reflection of his or her culture. Often, we can identify someone's heritage by the clothes they wear. For example, moccasins and fringed garments are used in some traditional Native American dress. In modern-day American society, it takes both pride and courage to wear these visible symbols of one's cultural background.

Complete one or more of the following activities to help you become more aware of traditional dress in various cultures.

Activity A: Here is a sample list of traditional clothing items from various cultures. Determine the cultures from which the item originated by using encyclopedias and other reference materials.

- kepah
- babushka
- sari
- turban

- kimono
- grass skirt
- sombrero

- mantilla
- kilt
- beret

Activity B: Share with your class an article of clothing or an accessory which reflects your cultural heritage. Be prepared to explain its significance to your classmates.

The Rosen Family: Courageous Pilgrims

In the novel *Number the Stars*, the Rosen family flees their homeland in pursuit of religious freedom. Likewise, the Pilgrims came to America seeking religious freedom. Both groups displayed tremendous courage in their actions as they both ventured forth into new lands.

Complete one of the following activities to help you think more about the courage of pilgrims.

Activity A: Consider how the flights of the Pilgrims and the Rosens are the same and different, then write an essay comparing and contrasting the two groups.

Activity B: The Pilgrims experienced many fears and encountered numerous obstacles when they came to the New World; the Rosens must have also encountered some of the same feelings and experiences when they arrived in Sweden. Imagine the inner strength both groups demonstrated. Work with a partner to brainstorm the types of fears and obstacles these people faced. Organize your ideas using the following chart:

Pilgrims		The Rosen Family	
Fears	Obstacles	Fears	Obstacles

Now that you have completed the chart, circle the fears and obstacles shared by both groups. Are you surprised by the similarities? What conclusions can you draw from this exercise?

Activity C: Even today, individuals sometimes seek a haven for practicing their beliefs. Almost since its inception, the United States has provided a sanctuary for such people. The Statue of Liberty is a beacon of hope for those people who have experienced persecution in their homelands. What other signs and symbols stand for courage? Create a collage showing them.

Land of Immigrants

In *Number the Stars*, the Rosen family escaped to a new land with hope for a better life. Throughout history many other families—probably your own relatives—came to America with the same dream. In fact, twelve million immigrants came to America through a small island located in Upper New York called Ellis Island between 1895-1924. Imagine the tremendous emotions the new immigrants experienced as they arrived at Ellis Island to begin their new lives in America. What courage these people displayed!

Complete one or both of the following activities to find out more about immigration.

Activity A: Investigate your own family's history and describe their journey to the United States. You may wish to include facts such as the date they arrived, the means of transportation they used, and why they left their homeland. If tracing your roots is not possible, ask a friend or neighbor to detail his or her family's arrival. Share your findings with your class.

Activity B: Imagine that you are a courageous immigrant setting foot on Ellis Island for the very first time. Write a letter describing your thoughts and impressions of America to a friend or relative in your homeland. Express the fears and hopes you are experiencing as you begin a new life.

Creating Your Own Town

When the Pilgrims journeyed to the New World, a vast wilderness awaited them. Their new lives would be much different from the ones they led in the established English towns they left behind. The Pilgrims' task was a great one, as they were forced to organize new towns and implement new governments. Although they used their British heritage as a model for their new homeland, they also needed to formulate and incorporate brand new ideas.

Now it's your turn to create a new town. Complete one of the following activities to learn more about designing a completely new place to live. Before you begin either activity, create cooperative learning groups of four to five students. Then, imagine that you have just landed in an unexplored territory.

Activity A: Work together to create your new town. Draw a rough sketch of the types of streets, buildings, and recreational areas you would include in your town. Be sure it is laid out in a practical and workable fashion; for example, would it be a good idea to place an amusement park next to a church or temple? Here are some possibilities that you may wish to include in designing your town:

- post office
- police department
- fire department
- bank
- town hall
- school
- senior center
- shopping areas

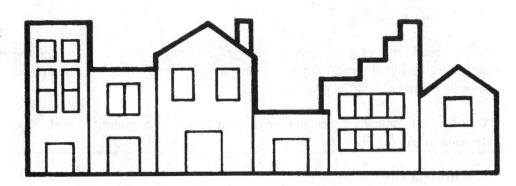

Activity B: In order for a town to run efficiently, certain rules and regulations must be in place. This is the job of the town government. Think about the type of government you would like in your town. Would you structure your government in a traditional manner? Would you include a mayor, town council, and community representatives? Would they have to meet any specific requirements? Would they be elected or appointed? Then list ten laws that you would enforce in your community.

1. _____
2. _____
3. _____
4. _____
5. _____
6. _____
7. _____
8. _____
9. _____
10. _____

Creating Your Own Town *(cont.)*

Answer the following questions in a class discussion:

- Was it easy to come to a consensus about the government?

- What lessons have you learned about establishing rules or laws?

- Are the rules or laws fair to all citizens?

- Are the rules or laws you created already in existence in your town, or did you create original concepts?

Activity C: Every town has its own identity, reflected by the special characteristics unique to each community. Design or create the following items to create an identity for a new town.

- Specify the name of the town

- Create a town motto

- Draw a town flag

Then, research the origins of the following metropolitan areas to find out the significance of their names and to list any nicknames or mottoes that identify them: Chicago, Los Angeles, New York, Detroit, Houston, Seattle, and Boston.

Activity D: Contact a representative of your local government to speak about your town or city. Here are some ideas for discussion.

- town or city history

- architecture and design within the town or city

- population changes of the town or city

- the origin and design of the flag and motto

- special resources

- city or town government

Activity E: Take a field trip to your local town hall, courthouse, or other governmental agency and notice the various government offices that are necessary to run a community. Think about the following questions while you are on the field trip:

- What is your role in government?

- Can middle school students make a difference in your community? How?

The Courage to Survive, Part I:

Island of the Blue Dolphins

Summary

In the opening scene of the novel *Island of the Blue Dolphins*, Karana and her brother, Ramo, are gathering plant roots on their island home which is located off the coast of California. When they look up, they see the red flags of Aleutian ships, and the peaceful existence they and their tribe have known is about to change forever.

The Russian ship's captain has come to negotiate a deal with Chief Chowig (Karana and Ramo's father) that would allow them to hunt the otters that dwell on the island. Although Chief Chowig is initially suspicious, he and Captain Orlav arrive at an agreement.

But as the hunt continues, the tribe comes to believe that the Russians are not honoring their end of the bargain. When Chief Chowig confronts Captain Orlav and his crew, a battle ensues, resulting both in his own death and the death of many others in the tribe.

After these tragic events, the newly elected chief decides it is best for the tribe to leave the island and seek refuge elsewhere. But when the ship destined for the new homeland leaves the island, Karana realizes that Ramo is not on board. In a valiant attempt to retrieve her brother, Karana dives into the water and swims ashore, but she is too late. The ship departs, leaving the siblings stranded on the Island of the Blue Dolphins.

As Karana and Ramo prepare for their life alone on the island, tragedy strikes again when Ramo is attacked and killed by a pack of wild dogs. Now Karana is truly alone with no one to turn to in a crisis. In addition, because the women of the tribe traditionally did not learn many of the tasks related to survival, Karana must depend on her own ingenuity and skills. For example, Karana must learn to fashion and use weapons for hunting and protection.

Throughout the early years of her island adventure, Karana fears the pack of wild dogs that mauled and killed her brother and is determined to kill them, especially their leader. However, when the opportunity comes to destroy the leader, Karana spares its life. Karana names the dog Rontu, and it soon becomes her trusted companion, helping to ease Karana's longing for human companionship.

Karana and Rontu confront many challenges during their time on the island, such as earthquakes and tidal waves. In addition, both loneliness and the fear of the Aleuts' return continually haunt Karana. As trying as all these experiences are, they help transform Karana from a girl to a young woman.

At the conclusion of the story, Karana and her animal friends are rescued and transported to the Catholic mission in Santa Barbara.

Vocabulary List

Listed below are vocabulary words that will be helpful for you to know as you read *Island of the Blue Dolphins*. Use the vocabulary activities on page 14 to learn the meanings of these words. Write them here.

bale _____

ample _____

stern _____

ravine _____

omen _____

shimmered _____

lair _____

utensils _____

sinews _____

plank _____

reef _____

barbed _____

haunch _____

crouch _____

stunted _____

crevice _____

grasp _____

oblong _____

mesa _____

shuddered _____

Myths and Legends

Since ancient times, people have searched for an explanation of earthquakes, tidal waves (also known as tsunamis), and many other natural disasters. Because of recent discoveries, today we have scientific answers to many of our questions.

Primitive societies, however, relied on myths and legends for explanations. Most myths and legends were not written down but were passed down orally from one generation to the next. Only in recent times have many of these stories been recorded on paper.

In many myths, natural events were attributed to the activities of gods and goddesses; for example, if a god was angered by a mortal (human being), he created a punishment such as an earthquake, a tidal wave, volcanic eruptions, etc. It took great courage for mere mortals to challenge powerful mythological beings.

Complete one or more of the following activities to help you learn more about mythology.

Activity A: Research and summarize a myth in which a mortal challenges one of the gods. Illustrate your summary, then with your classmates create an art gallery in your classroom of mythological beings.

Activity B: In chapter 12 of *Island of the Blue Dolphins,* author Scott O'Dell refers to the creation myth of Karana's tribe. Have a volunteer locate and read aloud this myth from the novel. Paraphrase the myth in your own words, then draw your own picture of Tumaiyowat and Mukat. Compare the pictures you create with those drawn by your classmates.

Myths and Legends *(cont.)*

Activity C: Throughout the ages, people have pondered the question of how the world began, and most ancient cultures have creation myths to provide an explanation. Create five cooperative learning groups, then make each group responsible for learning about the creation myth from one of the following ancient cultures:

- Egyptian
- Greek
- Native American
- Roman
- Celtic

Have a representative from each group read aloud the culture's creation myth, then compare and contrast all of them. When you have finished this part of the activity, illustrate any gods or goddesses represented in your group's selected creation myth.

Activity D: Karana refers to the dolphins as being a "good omen." What is an omen? Find other examples of omens and their meanings in *Island of the Blue Dolphins*. Discuss them in class.

Next, consider the concept of superstitions. Make a list of any superstitions of which you may have heard or believe. Do you think it takes courage not to believe in superstitions? For example, does it take courage to defy the common superstition of not walking under a ladder or crossing the path of a black cat? Discuss this idea with your class.

Earth Sciences

Tornadoes, hurricanes, floods, earthquakes, volcanic eruptions—these are just a sampling of the power of nature. Are you a survivor of one of nature's mighty forces? In *Island of the Blue Dolphins*, Karana courageously confronts the challenges of island life, in particular, ocean forces, a tidal wave, and an earthquake. Read on to learn more about each of these natural occurrences.

Ocean Forces

As Karana navigates her small canoe on the large expanse of ocean in Chapter 10, she has the following experience: "At dusk I looked back. The island of the Blue Dolphins had disappeared. This is the first time I felt afraid." Karana's fears originate from her realization that because of nature's awesome power, a calm ocean can quickly generate dangerous waves.

The ocean tremendously affects and is affected by the forces of nature. Three-quarters of the Earth's surface is covered with water; in fact, all seven of Earth's continents can fit into the Pacific Ocean. And, of course, the Earth is the only planet that has oceans at all.

Where did the oceans come from? One theory states that billions of years ago, gases rose from the Earth's hot crust. As the gases and land cooled, the deep troughs on the Earth's surface filled with water. (Remember, steam turns into water when cooled.) Another theory suggests that volcanic rock slowly released steam water over many billions of years, which again cooled and formed Earth's oceans.

Earth Science *(cont.)*

Ocean Forces *(cont.)*

Complete one or both of the following activities to learn more about oceans.

Activity A: List the five oceans found on Earth on the lines below.

_____

_____

_____

_____

Now research the following:

1. What is the scientific term for the study of the oceans?

2. Which is the largest ocean?

3. Which is the deepest ocean?

4. What is the chemical composition of ocean water?

5. Some scientists do not classify the Antarctic Ocean as a true ocean. Why?

Activity B: Ocean waters are always moving in huge streams called currents. Currents are caused by many things, such as wind, the rotation of the Earth, and tides caused by the moon's pull of gravity. One interesting fact about currents is that they move in large, circulating loops of water called *gores*. In the northern hemisphere, gores move in a clock-wise direction that keeps warm water moving toward the cool, polar areas and cool water moving toward the equator; in the southern hemisphere, gores move counter-clockwise. Thus, in both hemispheres ocean currents affect the climate of nearby regions.

Now define the following terms using a dictionary or an encyclopedia: clock-wise, counter-clockwise, hemisphere, polar, equator, tide, rotation, circulating.

Earth Sciences (cont.)

The Power of Tidal Waves

In the novel, Karana experiences the awesome power of a tidal wave which destroys her painstaking preparations for the winter ahead. A tidal wave, also known by the Japanese term *tsunami,* can be a devastating force of nature. When the energy of a wave moves along a fault in the ocean floor, the beginning of a tsunami occurs. If it meets land, this energy becomes compressed and a tidal wave is created. This wave may be 50-100 feet high and have a velocity (speed and direction) of 600 mph. A tsunami can travel thousands of miles from its point of origin. Modern scientific equipment can predict the length, speed, and direction of tsunamis. In some parts of the world, emergency warnings to evacuate can be issued. Unfortunately, Karana did not have modern devices to warn her of danger.

Complete the following activity to learn more about tidal waves.

Activity: In Chapter 27, Scott O'Dell describes the approaching tidal wave in the following manner:

> *The air was suddenly tight around me. There was a faint sound as if some giant animal were sucking the air in and out through its teeth. The rumbling came closer out of an empty sky, filling my ears. Then beyond the gleam of the beach and the bare rocks and reefs, more than a league beyond them, I saw a great white crest moving down upon the island.*
>
> *It seemed to move slowly between the sea and the sky, but it was the sea itself. I tore off the shields I wore over my eyes. In terror I ran along the sand split. I ran and stumbled and got up and ran again. The sand shuddered under my feet as the first wave struck. Spray fell around me like rain. It was filled with pieces of kelp and small fish.*

If only Karana had known of the approaching tidal wave, she could have been better prepared. List five things that you think she might have done to prevent the destruction she experienced.

1. _____

2. _____

3. _____

4. _____

5. _____

Earth Sciences *(cont.)*

Earthquakes

One of the primary causes of tidal waves occurs when an earthquake takes place beneath the ocean floor. However, earthquakes also originate on land due to volcanic eruptions, landslides, and faulting, or the shifting of the earth's plates. In the opening sentence of Chapter 28, Scott O'Dell writes, "The earthquake did little damage." This is due to the fact that the island was undeveloped; i.e., there were no bridges or buildings, etc., which could have been demolished in a quake.

Being in an earthquake of any size is a frightening experience. When the Earth begins to tremble, there is no way to predict how long or how severe the earthquake will be. Although most earthquakes last less than one minute, they can cause much devastation. Entire towns and cities have been destroyed by some earthquakes. After the quake stops, smaller shaking or aftershocks may still occur.

One of the most violent earthquakes recorded in North America took place in Anchorage, Alaska, in 1964. However, the loss of property and lives was not great because it occurred in an underpopulated area of the world. Other earthquakes not as violent as the one described above, were responsible for more damage simply because of their locations.

The *magnitude* of an earthquake is measured on an instrument known as the Richter Scale, but the intensity of the quake cannot be recorded by a machine. *Intensity* is determined instead by eyewitness accounts and professional damage inspection. An earthquake has only one Richter magnitude but may have many intensities.

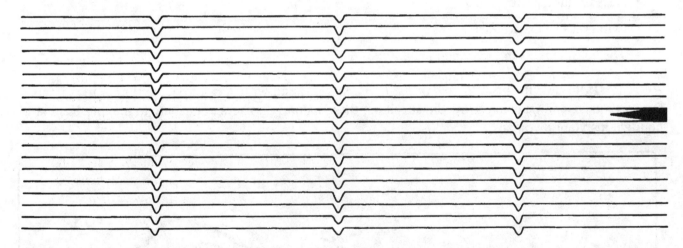

Earthquake waves are measured in a different manner. Chang Heng, a Chinese scientist living in 200 A.D., created the first instrument to record earthquakes. Today, scientists refer to this device as a *seismoscope*. Centuries later, in 1856, Luigi Palmieri invented a more accurate device for recording earthquakes called a *seismograph*.

Earth Sciences *(cont.)*

Earthquakes *(cont.)*

Choose one of the following activities to help you learn more about earthquakes.

Activity A: Research and write a report which includes diagrams on the inventions of Chang Heng and Luigi Palmieri.

Activity B: Today the Richter Scale is used worldwide to study earthquakes. Brainstorm five questions you want to know about Charles F. Richter and his invention, then find answers to your questions in the school library or learning center.

Activity C: There have been many devastating earthquakes throughout history. For example, in Lisbon, Portugal, in 1775, an earthquake destroyed seventy-five percent of the buildings in that city and a resulting tidal wave destroyed the city's harbor. The causalties totaled more than ten thousand people.

Create cooperative learning groups of three to four students and select a major earthquake to research. Find out the following information using your learning center:

- Date

- Location

- Extent of property damage

- Loss of human life

- Duration of the earthquake

- The earthquake's intensity and magnitude

Activity D: Review the novel *Island of the Blue Dolphins* and write a brief description of the effects of the earthquake and tsunami. How did surviving these natural disasters contribute to making Karana a courageous young woman?

Ocean-o-"graph"-y

Now that you know about the oceans, let's put your math skills to work. One form of physical representation used by mathematicians is the graph. There are many different types of graphs, including line, bar, and pie graphs. Take a close look at pie and bar graphs in reference to the ocean.

A pie graph begins with the idea that the area within a drawn circle represents 100% of something. The circle is then cut or sliced into sections just like a pie, with each "slice" representing a fractional part of the whole. Your task is to create a pie graph which represents the space filled by each of four oceans. Here is an example: If there are 20 children in your class, 12 boys and 8 girls, the pie graph would look like this:

Boys

$$\frac{12}{20} = \frac{3}{5}$$

$$5 \overline{)\begin{array}{c} .6 \\ 3.0 \\ \underline{3.0} \\ 0 \end{array}}$$

To find percentage, multiply by 100:

$$\begin{array}{r} 100 \\ \times\ 0.6 \\ \hline 60.0\ = 60\% \end{array}$$

Girls

$$\frac{8}{20} = \frac{2}{5}$$

$$5 \overline{)\begin{array}{c} .4 \\ 2.0 \\ \underline{2.0} \\ 0 \end{array}}$$

To find percentage, multiply by 100:

$$\begin{array}{r} 100 \\ \times\ 0.4 \\ \hline 40.0\ = 40\% \end{array}$$

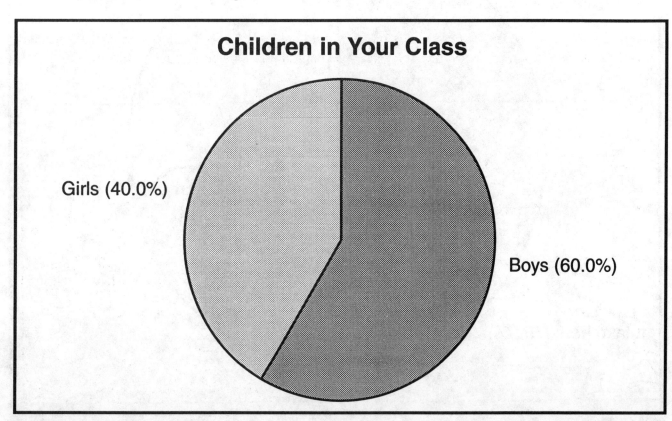

Children in Your Class

Girls (40.0%)

Boys (60.0%)

Ocean-o- "graph"-y *(cont.)*

Use the information from this example to complete a pie graph showing the area of earth's five oceans in square miles. The chart below displays in square miles the percentage of each ocean compared to the total of all oceans combined. Finish the pie graph using this information. The portion of the graph pertaining to the Atlantic Ocean has already been completed.

Ocean	Percent of Total Area in Sq. Miles
Atlantic	24.5%
Pacific	49.3%
Indian	22.0%
Arctic	4.2%

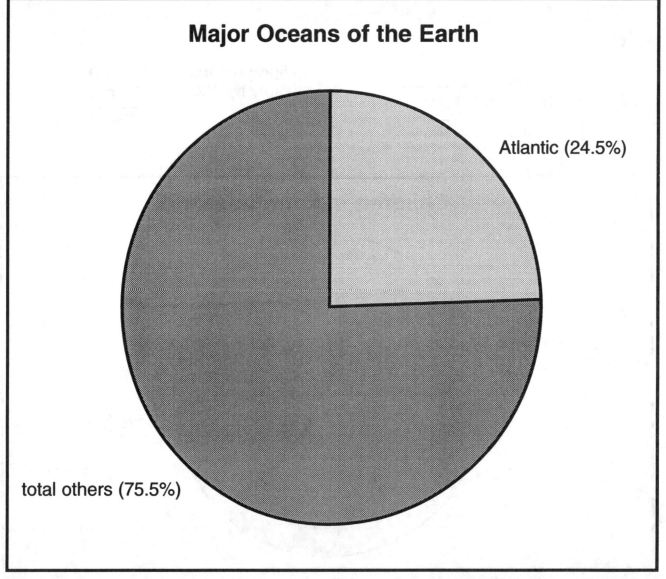

Major Oceans of the Earth

Atlantic (24.5%)

total others (75.5%)

Ocean-o- "graph"-y *(cont.)*

Now, transfer the information from the pie graph to a bar graph by drawing a bar up to the percentage that corresponds to the data provided for each ocean. Once again, information about the Atlantic Ocean has already been graphed.

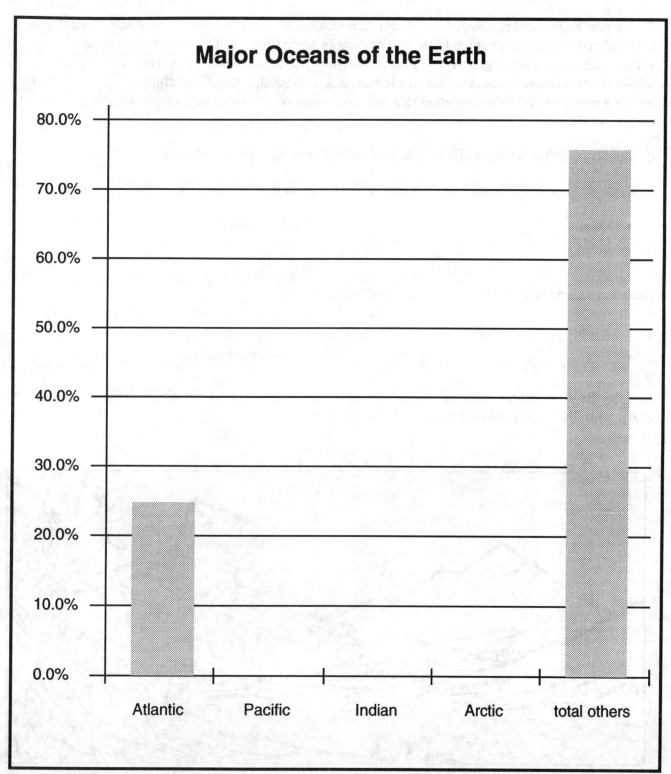

The Biosphere

The term **biosphere** refers to the oceans, land, and the part of the atmosphere occupied by life. From the ocean floor to the highest strata of the atmosphere where life can be found, the biosphere stretches 21 kilometers.

The largest major land regions of the biosphere are called *biomes*. A biome is uniquely characterized by its climate, its *fauna* or animal life, and its *flora* or vegetation. Within each biome there exist various *habitats*, or small geographical areas, in which plant and animal life exists. For example, within the rain forest biome, the toucan's habitat is a fruit-bearing tree. The climate, flora, and fauna within a biome are all linked together in a web of dependency. In this way, nature keeps all living things in balance.

Complete the following activities to help you learn more about the biosphere.

Activity A: Create four investigative teams with each team investigating one of the following biomes:

- Desert
- Savanna

- Rain forest
- Tundra

Each team member must then research one of the following:

- Climate
- Flora

- Fauna
- Geographical features

Activity B: When all the research has been completed, illustrate the biome with its various features. Make your illustration colorful to bring the biome to life.

The Biosphere *(cont.)*

Activity C: Maintaining the four investigative teams, brainstorm how Karana's life would have been different if she had lived in the biome you have investigated. Create a chart to categorize the information, using the chart below as a guide.

Diet	
Shelter	
Forces of Nature	
Natural Resources (animal, plant life, etc.)	

Activity D: Now it is time to use your imagination by rewriting a scene from *Island of the Blue Dolphins*, placing Karana in the biome you have researched.

Activity E: Make a mobile depicting your biome. Include both the flora and the fauna of the geographical area. You will need a clothes hanger, some string or fish line, and pictures that you either have clipped from magazines or created and glued onto shapes made from colored construction paper. Be sure your mobile is balanced before hanging it for display.

Ecology

In *Island of the Blue Dolphins*, Karana utilizes the island's resources wisely. For example, she uses whale bones to construct a fence to protect her house and to fashion spears from the remains of the sea elephant. Karana and her tribe were very resourceful people.

What does it mean to be resourceful? A natural resource is an important material found in nature. These resources are essential for people's survival. Some of these include air, plants, animals, water, soil, and metals. Being resourceful means using these materials creatively and efficiently to fill one's needs.

Complete one or more of the following activities to help you learn about natural resources and ecology.

Activity A: Think of three ways Karana and her tribe effectively used items within their environment in order to survive on the island.

1. _____

2. _____

3. _____

Activity B: Karana's tribe understands the idea that natural resources are limited. Modern people, however, have become wasteful and disrespectful of the environment. Only recently has awareness grown concerning the preservation of our resources. Fortunately, many resources can be used again and again if they are recycled, i.e., collected and treated in order to be reused.

Using a dictionary and encyclopedia and other resource materials, define each of these terms that are associated with recycling:

- compost _____
- ore _____
- feedstock _____
- mineral _____
- fossil fuel _____
- conservation _____

- fertile _____
- landfill _____
- reforestation _____
- native metal _____
- desalination _____
- pollutants _____

Ecology *(cont.)*

Activity C: Recyclable materials include glass bottles, aluminum cans, and newspapers. As a class project, organize a recycling campaign. Consider the following ideas:

- How can you increase environmental awareness at your school?

- How can you motivate others to pitch in and improve the environment?

Be courageous and remind individuals who are not recycling to lend a helping hand. No contribution is too small if it helps save our planet.

Activity D: If your town has a recycling center, contact it and invite a representative to visit your school. Prepare a list of questions and concerns you may have regarding recycling in your town. If you do not have a recycling center where you live, write to your local government officials to see if one can be started.

Activity E: Plan a field trip to your local recycling center, landfill, or other environmental agency or organization. Find out what people there are doing to preserve the environment.

Geography

Every geographical region has particular challenges that its inhabitants must endure in order to survive. In *Island of the Blue Dolphins*, the reader finds Karana, the heroine, in many situations in which she must fight for survival. She must brave the climate, the landscape, the wildlife, and the forces of nature associated with an island environment. Karana must also stockpile food to prepare for winter.

In the chart below, categorize the environmental conditions found on San Nicolas Island—the real "Island of the Blue Dolphins." Scan the novel to help you fill in the chart. An example is provided for each category.

Forces of Nature	Climate	Geographical features	Wildlife	Vegetation
Tsunami	Winds	Caves	Sea Elephants	Roots

Observation: An Important Tool of Science

An observation is a fact you can notice. For example, you might observe that a baseball is round, a bat is made of wood, and the infield of a baseball field is shaped like a diamond.

Scientists use observation to gather and record information about a given subject. From their observations, scientists explore ideas, ask questions, and draw conclusions. Observation is very important to a scientist, whether it is done in a laboratory or in a natural setting.

Courage is an abstract concept and cannot be studied in a laboratory or examined under a microscope. However, individual acts of courage can be observed if you look closely at the world around you.

Complete the following activities to learn about observing acts of courage.

Activity A: In the novel *Island of the Blue Dolphins*, Karana displays many acts of courage while trying to survive. Record five of her courageous actions on the lines below.

1. _____

2. _____

3. _____

4. _____

5. _____

Activity B: For the next ten days, pretend you are a social scientist. Carefully observe the world around you. Take note of the actions of your principal, teachers, fellow classmates, friends, and family. Record any acts of courage that you observe, no matter how small, in a journal. For instance, did you observe a crossing guard stopping traffic on a busy street to help younger children safely cross? Did you notice a fellow student help settle a dispute at recess? Record the details of each act of courage.

Women of Courage

In the novel *Island of the Blue Dolphins*, Karana performs various tasks traditionally accomplished by men in her tribe, such as creating weapons to use against wild dogs and other creatures, in order to survive. Even so, the consequences of going against tribal tradition worry her:

> *As I lay there, I wondered what would happen to me if I went against the law of our tribe which forbade the making of weapons by women. . . Would the four winds blow in from the four directions of the world and smother me as I made the weapons? Or would the earth tremble, as many said and bury me beneath the falling rocks? Or, as others said, would the sea rise over the island in a terrible flood?*

Despite her fears, Karana goes against tradition and constructs the weapons and other items she needs to survive.

In the modern world we also find many courageous women who have broken with society's accepted ways and challenged stereotypes, that is, fixed or unchangeable ways of looking at things. Elizabeth Blackwell, Sandra Day O'Connor, and Sally Ride are three examples of women who have challenged society's stereotypes. Meet these three women of courage on the following pages.

Sally Ride　　　　　　　　*Sandra Day O'Connor*

Elizabeth Blackwell

Calling Dr. Blackwell!

"Code Blue! All available medical personnel, please report to the emergency room immediately!" Whereas once only male doctors would have answered this page, today doctors of both genders answer it. But not long ago, the medical profession had stereotyped roles—men became doctors; women became nurses. When women were finally accepted to and graduated from medical school, they were viewed with suspicion and distrust. Imagine the courage it required to tear down the walls of discrimination and prejudice.

Elizabeth Blackwell (1821-1910) was the first woman in the United States to obtain a degree from medical school when she graduated from Geneva Medical School in 1849. Her many accomplishments included the establishment of the New York Infirmary for Women and Children in 1857. She also aided in the founding of the London School of Medicine in England (her native country) in 1869. Because of her ground-breaking achievements in medicine, the Blackwell Medal of Recognition has been awarded to outstanding women physicians annually since 1949.

Elizabeth Blackwell

Choose one of the following activities to help acquaint you with Dr. Blackwell and the stereotypes that existed at the time she went into the field of medicine.

Activity A: If you were transported to the year 1849 and had the opportunity to meet Dr. Blackwell, what three questions would you like her to answer?

1. _____

2. _____

3. _____

Activity B: Assume you are a male fellow classmate of the future Dr. Blackwell at Geneva Medical School. Keeping in mind the prejudices against women at this time in history, write a paragraph describing your reaction to having a woman in your class. Would you be supportive or prejudiced? Choose one of these positions before you begin to write.

Activity C: Assume you are on the Board of Admissions of Geneva Medical College. Would you elect to admit Elizabeth Blackwell as an incoming student? Why or why not? Develop a persuasive speech highlighting main reasons for or against her admission and argue your stand to your fellow "board members." (Note: Your ideas may or may not reflect your personal feelings regarding these assignments.)

Sandra Day O'Connor: Supreme Court Justice

The Supreme Court—the highest court in our land—is composed of nine members: one Chief Justice and eight associate justices. The function of the Supreme Court is to help "lower" courts to interpret and understand how the laws of our land operate. Supreme Court justices are appointed by the President and approved by Congress. Despite the fact that the Supreme Court has been in existence since the early days of our government's existence, it was not until 1981 that a woman was nominated by President Ronald Reagan—Sandra Day O'Connor.

Justice O'Connor was born in El Paso, Texas, on March 26, 1930. She served in the Arizona State Senate from 1972-1974, then became a judge for the Arizona Supreme Court in 1974-1979. She next served on the Arizona Court of Appeals from 1979-1981. Justice O'Connor demonstrated remarkable courage in accepting a prestigious position that had never before been held by a woman.

Choose one of the following activities to find out more about the Supreme Court.

Activity A: Several famous cases have been tried in the Supreme Court in our nation's history. Many courageous decisions made by the justices have had a significant impact on our lives. Create cooperative learning groups of three students, then go to the school library or learning center to research one of the following landmark cases: *Brown v. The Board of Education*; *Miranda v. Arizona*; and *U.S. v. Nixon*. Then answer the following questions:

1. What was the main issue of the case?_____

   _____

2. Who was involved? _____

   _____

3. What was the outcome?_____

   _____

4. Why was it a courageous decision?_____

   _____

Sandra Day O'Connor: Supreme Court Justice *(cont.)*

Activity B: Traditionally, Karana's tribe did not permit women to perform certain tasks. Unfortunately, discrimination against women existed in our society until recently. Despite graduating *magna cum laude* (with great distinction) and ranking third in her class at Stanford University, Justice O'Connor had difficulty obtaining a position as a lawyer. When she initially sought employment, Justice O'Connor was offered secretarial work. Justice O'Connor's perseverance to excel in her profession demonstrates that she is a courageous woman. In paragraph form, explain how Justice O'Connor serves as an inspirational role model for anyone pursuing a dream despite tremendous odds.

Activity C: Write a letter to Justice O'Connor expressing some concerns you may have about laws or legal issues in your community. You may wish to write the letter individually or as a class project. Here is the address:

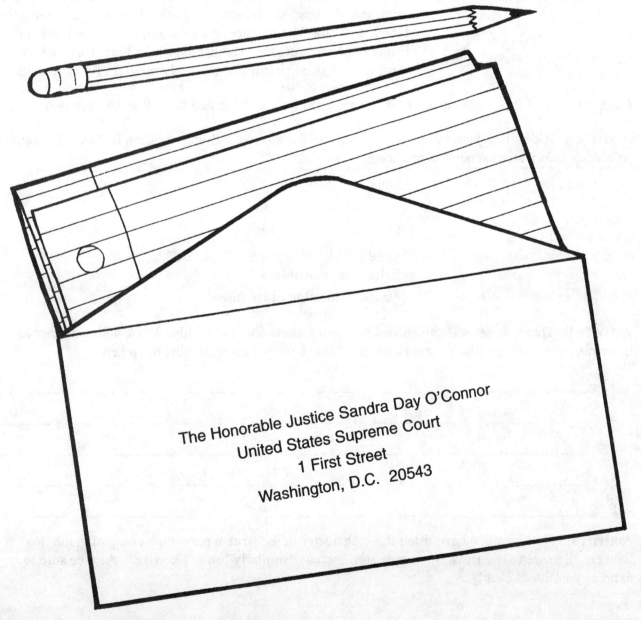

The Honorable Justice Sandra Day O'Connor
United States Supreme Court
1 First Street
Washington, D.C. 20543

Sally Ride: First Woman Astronaut

"Five, four, three, two, one. Ignition! We have lift off."

This familiar phrase signals that yet another journey into outer space has begun, a thrilling and courageous endeavor. Very few individuals have the courage to become an astronaut. One member of this elite group is Sally Kirsten Ride, the first female astronaut.

Sally Ride

Like Karana in *Island of the Blue Dolphins*, Ride accepted challenges traditionally faced only by men. Her accomplishments mark "one giant step for womankind!"

Ride was born on May 26, 1951. She earned a Ph.D. in physics from Stanford University in 1977, a degree that provided her with the required knowledge to become a member of the flight crew on Space Shuttle missions in 1983 and 1984. After completing these missions, she headed a ten-member study team formed to map out future goals for 21st-century space exploration. Two ideas the team suggested were the establishment of a lunar base and the creation of a strong earth science study program for astronauts.

Complete one of the following activities to learn more about Ride and her job as an astronaut.

Activity A: Ride's first journey into space was the seventh space shuttle mission in 1983. Research the following information about this mission:

> Date
> Location of take off site
> Objective of the mission
> Length of flight
> Fellow crew members
> Date and location of landing

Activity B: There are several similarities between Karana and Sally Ride. Work with a partner to determine the qualities which these two remarkable heroines share and list them here:

1. _____
2. _____
3. _____
4. _____
5. _____

Activity C: Now that you have listed these character traits, write a paragraph comparing the two women. Be sure to use terms of comparison, such as "similarly" and "likewise." Also be sure to express your ideas clearly.

Karana's Diary

Write down what you believe Karana's responses might be to the following scenes from the novel:

Seeing Captain Orlav kill her father
_____
_____

Watching Ramo being left behind
_____
_____

Finding Ramo's mauled body
_____
_____

Spending her first night alone
_____
_____

Confronting the wild dogs
_____
_____

Making friends with Rontu
_____
_____

Fighting the devil fish
_____
_____

Exchanging gifts with Tutok
_____
_____

Exploring the scary cave
_____
_____

Being rescued
_____
_____

Discovering what happened to her family
_____
_____

Creating a Diorama

Throughout *Island of the Blue Dolphins*, Scott O'Dell provides the reader with images of the island. Although everyone reads the same text, each person will create a different image of the island in his or her mind's eye. Express your own vision of the island by creating a diorama. Pay attention to the details described by the author in order to bring his words to life.

Materials:

- shoe box
- fabric
- tin foil
- rocks, sea shells, and other objects associated with island life
- small models of animals

- human figurines
- tape
- glue
- markers
- paints

Tips on constructing a successful diorama:

1. Create a backdrop on the rear surface of the shoe box. You may wish to use paint, markers, or fabric for this task.

2. Create a three-dimensional scene by placing objects in the box, i.e., a small rubber dolphin, a rock, or a cave made of clay. These objects should reflect the scene you have selected from the novel.

3. Let your imagination soar!

Writing a Picture Book

When you were a small child, chances are your favorite story came from a picture book. Picture books often take a complex plot and transform it into a story that retains important details. There are also illustrations which correspond to the text and add to the story's meaning.

Choose one of the following activities to create your own picture book manuscript and illustrations.

Activity A: Turn the novel *Island of the Blue Dolphins* into a picture book by briefly summarizing the story in ten to fifteen pages, with no more than one or two sentences per page. Each page should include a picture which depicts the action of a major event of the novel. Here are steps to help you.

> **Step 1:**   List 10–15 events which you think develop the plot of the novel.
>
> **Step 2**:   Summarize each event in one to two sentences.
>
> **Step 3:**   Draw a picture to illustrate each event, remembering to leave room to write or paste in your text.
>
> **Step 4:**   Color each drawing.
>
> **Step 5:**   Make a cover for the book and bind it together using appropriate materials.
>
> **Step 6:**   Share your book with a classmate and/or a younger child.

Activity B: Create an original picture book that features a main character who exhibits courage. Perhaps the main character can overcome obstacles similar to those faced by Karana in *Island of the Blue Dolphins*. Be sure to include an author page telling important facts about you.

Activity C: Bring your favorite picture book to school and read it to your class, then tell why this book is special to you. Your teacher may wish to display the class's collection on a separate shelf in the classroom.

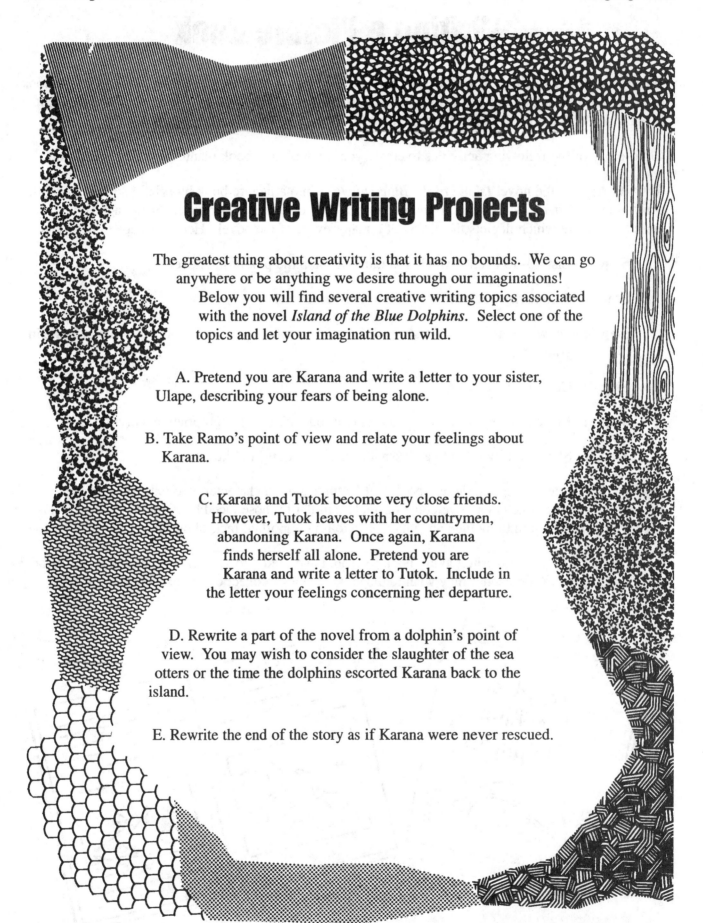

Creative Writing Projects

The greatest thing about creativity is that it has no bounds. We can go anywhere or be anything we desire through our imaginations! Below you will find several creative writing topics associated with the novel *Island of the Blue Dolphins*. Select one of the topics and let your imagination run wild.

A. Pretend you are Karana and write a letter to your sister, Ulape, describing your fears of being alone.

B. Take Ramo's point of view and relate your feelings about Karana.

C. Karana and Tutok become very close friends. However, Tutok leaves with her countrymen, abandoning Karana. Once again, Karana finds herself all alone. Pretend you are Karana and write a letter to Tutok. Include in the letter your feelings concerning her departure.

D. Rewrite a part of the novel from a dolphin's point of view. You may wish to consider the slaughter of the sea otters or the time the dolphins escorted Karana back to the island.

E. Rewrite the end of the story as if Karana were never rescued.

Surviving an Obstacle Course

Karana endured many physical challenges on the *Island of the Blue Dolphins*. Here's a chance to challenge your physical skills by running an obstacle course. Below you will find some suggestions to follow. You and your classmates may also wish to add some ideas of your own.

Suggested materials for creating an obstacle course:

- six traffic cones
- eight tires
- one basketball
- stop watch

- two boxes (provide several different sized shoe boxes)
- one hula hoop
- one mat
- one balance beam or a 2" x 4" (5 cm x 10 cm) piece of wood balanced on two cinder blocks

Station One: Set the six cones down three feet apart. Run in a weaving motion in between the cones; if you knock one down, you must begin again.

Station Two: Create a 20-foot (6 m) long straight course. Then place an appropriately sized box on each of your feet and walk the course from start to finish.

Station Three: Create a second straight course and on it place the tires side by side in pairs. Be sure that you place one foot in each tire as you run through this station.

Station Four: Spin the hula hoop around your waist ten times.

Station Five: Jump rope for one minute.

Station Six: Stand at the free-throw line on a basketball court and make 2 baskets. (You may wish to set a 30-second time limit.)

Station Seven: On mats, complete this series of exercises: 5 somersaults, 5 sit-ups, 5 push ups; and 5 jumping jacks.

Station Eight: Walk across the balance beam or piece of lumber without falling. Begin again if you fall.

The Courage to Survive, Part II:

Hatchet

Summary

In Gary Paulsen's popular novel *Hatchet*, the true spirit of courage and adventure are captured. The drama unfolds when the plane carrying the main character, Brian Robeson, crashes in the Canadian wilderness after the pilot suffers a fatal heart attack. Completely alone, Brian faces the physical, mental, and emotional challenges of this unfamiliar environment. He must also deal with the confusion and anger he feels about his parents' recent divorce.

Brian may have survived the plane crash, but his problems are just beginning. He is not prepared for hunger, thirst, wildlife, and weather conditions. Once he realizes that he may not be rescued, Brian begins to meet the challenges of his situation. He finds a suitable shelter and some bitter berries on which he feasts. Unused to such a diet, he becomes violently ill and realizes that he must be careful about what he eats. But when he later finds some luscious raspberries, he also discovers something else that enjoys the sweet fruit—a bear. After successfully avoiding a confrontation with this animal, Brian returns to his shelter where he encounters a porcupine. The porcupine shoots quills into Brian's leg that are very painful to remove.

Needing to rest from this ordeal, Brian falls into a deep sleep and dreams about a cookout fire, triggering a memory of the hatchet his mother had given him before his trip. When he awakens he remembers the hatchet's usefulness in chopping wood for a fire. Igniting a real fire also "lights a fire" within Brian, who accepts his new home and learns to hunt and fish for food.

One day Brian hears a plane flying overhead; unfortunately, the plane's pilot does not spot him. Brian's hope slowly turns to despair, and he attempts suicide using the hatchet. When this attempt fails, he realizes his foolishness and his will to survive strengthens.

Brian continues to have various run-ins, but now these events only help build his resolve to survive. With a new attitude Brian decides to retrieve the survival pack from the plane's fuselage when it resurfaces from the lake during a storm. Obtaining the pack is a difficult task, and Brian temporarily misplaces the hatchet on which he depends. Brian's quest is successful, however, and the emergency bag yields items such as dehydrated food, a first-aid kit, and an emergency transmitter that Brian tosses aside with his belief that it will not work. But when a pilot reads its signal, this "useless" transmitter brings Brian his rescue.

At the end, Brian returns home more confident, more mature, and more understanding of his family situation.

Exploring the Wilderness

New vegetation, new terrain, and unfamiliar wildlife are just some of the challenges that Brian encounters in the Canadian wilds. Through the ages, various people have faced similar circumstances as they traveled uncharted lands and waters. These individuals are known as explorers. Like Brian in *Hatchet,* explorers often experienced great hardships in their struggle to survive. Examine some of the courageous individuals who participated in great voyages of exploration.

The Vikings

Many historians believe that the Vikings, not Columbus and his crew, were the first Europeans to reach the Americas. The Vikings were known as a group of ruthless people who came from the northern lands we now know as Norway, Sweden, and Denmark. From 800-1100 A.D., the Vikings were feared by others because many of them stole treasures from monasteries and enslaved young men and women. Many Viking explorations were motivated by a desire to find new opportunities for trade and to establish new colonies for their growing population.

Choose one of the following activities to help you learn more about the Viking explorers.

Activity A: Viking ships are still considered to be superior to all other sailing crafts constructed during that age. This is due in part to the Vikings' expertise in working with wood and metal. Research the design of Viking ships and write a brief, illustrated report on your findings.

Activity B: Research the exploits of the Vikings, focusing on notorious Vikings such as Eric the Red and his son, Leif Ericson. Then consider the idea that explorers are generally thought of as courageous individuals. Do the Vikings fit this definition? Why or why not? Write a paragraph detailing your thoughts, giving examples from your research to support your answer.

Exploring the Wilderness *(cont.)*

Christopher Columbus

Every October 12, we commemorate the historic voyage made by Cristobal Colon, or, as we know him, Christopher Columbus. Columbus believed that he could reach the Far East by sailing westward across the Atlantic Ocean from Europe. Although Columbus was a citizen of Portugal, he did not gain support there for his idea. Instead, Queen Isabella and King Ferdinand of Spain gave Columbus financial backing that enabled him to sail on his first voyage.

Based on existing maps, Columbus believed he had reached the Far East when his fleet landed in what later came to be called the New World. Because of this belief, he called the inhabitants of this new land *indios*; today, we use the English translation, "Indian." (Most tribespeople prefer the term Native American.) Columbus named the first island upon which he and his crew set foot "San Salvador," which translates as "the Savior," an appropriate name since one purpose of the voyage was to spread Christianity throughout the world. Columbus raised a cross on the shores of San Salvador as a symbolic gesture of his mission.

Complete Activity A, then choose from Activities B and C to learn more about Columbus and his voyage.

Activity A: On a map, trace Columbus' voyage of 1492-1493 that led to the discovery of the New World.

Activity B: Write a dialogue based on one of the following suggestions, being sure to address the fears and the courage that each group must have experienced in these situations:

- What Columbus and the natives might have said if they had been able to communicate

- What Columbus and his crew might have said when they spotted land after being at sea so long

- What the natives of San Salvador might have said to each other as they watched the approach of Columbus and his crew

Activity C: Put on a play by acting out your dialogues with classmates. You may wish to use costumes and props that reflect the times in which Columbus lived.

A Panel of Famous Explorers

As research reveals, explorers generally are brave people who dare to venture into the unknown, altering the course of history. Think how different our world would be if Christopher Columbus or Neil Armstrong had not been willing to risk their lives to explore new frontiers. Below you will discover a list highlighting the major accomplishments of four early explorers.

Ferdinand Magellan (1480-1521): Magellan was the first explorer to circumnavigate (sail around) the world. He gave the Pacific Ocean its name, and at the tip of Cape Horn in South Africa, a strait is named in honor of his being the first European explorer brave enough to sail through its rough waters.

Vasco Nunez de Balboa (1475-1519): Balboa's journeys took him across the isthmus of Panama in Central America, making him the first European to see the Pacific Ocean.

Francisco Pizarro (1476-1541): With 185 men and 27 horses, Pizarro conquered Peru's vast Inca empire in 1532.

Hernando Cortez (1485-1546): Cortez led an expedition to Mexico, where he captured the Aztec leader Montezuma and conquered the Aztec people, changing forever the lives of native people there and in Central America.

A Panel of Famous Explorers *(cont.)*

Complete one or more of the following activities to learn more about these explorers.

Activity A: Divide the class into four groups, with each group selecting one of the listed explorers to research. Try to find several historical facts that demonstrate the courage of this explorer. After completing this task, appoint a student from your group to assume the identity of your chosen explorer. Using the format outlined on pages 31–32, debate which of the four explorers was the most courageous. The class can then determine the winning explorer by casting secret ballots.

Activity B: Some of the four explorers can be thought of as conquerors, not explorers. In a class discussion, consider the following ideas: What is the difference between a conqueror and an explorer? Who do you think exhibits more courage?

Activity C: Each of the four men was a ship captain. Assume the identity of one of these courageous men and for one week keep a captain's log, or daily record, of the day's events and experiences. Think about the hardships these men may have endured and be sure to write about the physical, mental, and emotional problems faced by you and your crew.

Canada: The Taming of a Wilderness

In *Hatchet*, Brian Robeson must become an explorer, not by choice but by circumstance. However, there have been many men who willingly and courageously ventured into the Canadian wilderness, including John Cabot, Jacques Cartier, Samuel de Champlain, and Henry Hudson. These explorers experienced many of the same setbacks as Brian as they explored the country we now know as Canada.

Complete one of the following activities to help you learn more about early Canadian exploration and history.

Activity A: Canadian history has been carved out by many courageous adventurers who have been given tribute with place names. Some Canadian place names are listed below. Create five equal cooperative learning groups, with each group assigned one place name to research. Find the explorer for which the area was named and its corresponding location. Be prepared to present an oral report to the class and to point out the location on a map. (If a map is not available in your classroom, you may wish to reproduce the one on this page.)

A. Hudson Bay   D. Baffin Bay

B. Vancouver, British Columbia   E. Lake Champlain

C. Davis Strait

Canada: The Taming of a Wilderness *(cont.)*

Activity B: Just prior to being rescued, Brian relied on the modern conveniences and technological devices he found in the survival bag that he had retrieved from the plane, including a rifle, an aluminum cook set, a waterproof container, matches and a lighter, a knife with a compass, and a first aid kit. But most importantly of all, the bag contained an emergency transmitter that radioed Brian's distress call. A plane soaring overhead intercepted the message and pinpointed the spot where Brian was found. Without this modern survival kit, Brian quite possibly would have perished in the wilderness.

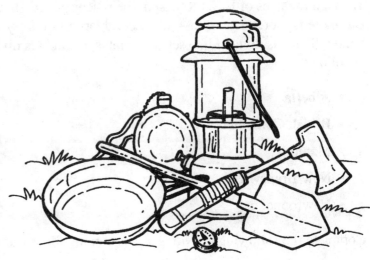

The early explorers probably carried a kit similar to Brian's during their expeditions. Consider the time in history in which these explorers lived, then list below ten items their emergency bags may have contained. Then compare this list with those found in Brian's emergency kit.

1. _____

2. _____

3. _____

4. _____

5. _____

6. _____

7. _____

8. _____

9. _____

10. _____

Exploring Canada

Through the eyes of Brian Robeson, the reader gets a glimpse of the immense Canadian wilderness. But there is more to Canada—that second largest country in the world—than wilderness. Just as the United States is divided into separate states, Canada is divided into ten provinces, or land regions, listed as follows:

- Alberta
- British Columbia
- Manitoba
- New Brunswick
- Newfoundland

- Nova Scotia
- Ontario
- Prince Edward Island
- Saskatchewan
- Quebec

Complete the following activities to learn more about Canadian provinces.

Activity A: Working with a partner, select and research a province. Present your findings in an illustrated booklet, making certain that you include the following information:

A. Highlights of its capital city

B. Population

C. Area in square miles and square kilometers

D. Year the region became a province

E. Geographical data: rivers, lakes, mountains/mountain ranges, etc.

F. Places of interest: museums, landmarks, national parks, etc.

G. Natural resources: plant and animal life, minerals, etc.

H. Industry and economy: imports and exports

I. Special features: official language, provincial floral and tree emblems, its coat of arms, its motto

J. Brief history of the province

K. Map

Activity B: Travel brochures from travel agencies and visitors bureaus feature the highlights of a geographical area. The brochures are written to attract tourists. Create a travel brochure on the province you have researched. List the major attractions of the area. Remember, give the brochure eye-appeal!

Brian's Courage

Throughout *Hatchet*, Brian proves he is a courageous young man. However, this does not mean that he is fearless. In the opening of Chapter 3, for example, just before the plane crashes Brian's thoughts scream, "Going to die, gonna die, gonna die." Likewise, he is also afraid when he encounters a bear while picking raspberries. In fact, Brian experiences fear many times within the pages of the novel.

Choose one of the following activities to explore the fears that Brian faces.

Activity A: Fill in the first column in the chart below with details from the novel that illustrate the times when Brian experiences fear, then record how Brian deals with these fears in the second column. An example has been provided.

Fear	Response
1. hunger	hoarding food
2.	
3.	
4.	
5.	

Activity B: Although "fear" and "courage" seem to be opposites, a closer look reveals that these two concepts often go hand in hand. For example, a soldier marching into battle must act courageously; however, he cannot help but fear for his life. Reflect on a time in your life when you experienced these seemingly conflicting emotions and then write a paragraph detailing this experience.

Activity C: What conclusion can you draw about courageous people based on Brian's ordeal? What insights, if any, have you gained in defining the meaning of "courage"?

Brian's Log

Although it would not be by choice, Brian Robeson of *Hatchet* also could be considered a daring explorer. If Brian had a pencil and paper, what entries do you think he would have recorded? Imagine that you are Brian and write sample entries below for the following scenes:

- Being swarmed by mosquitoes
- Meeting the bear
- Dropping the hatchet in the water

- Seeing the dead pilot underwater
- Witnessing the aftermath of the tornado
- Getting stuck by porcupine quills

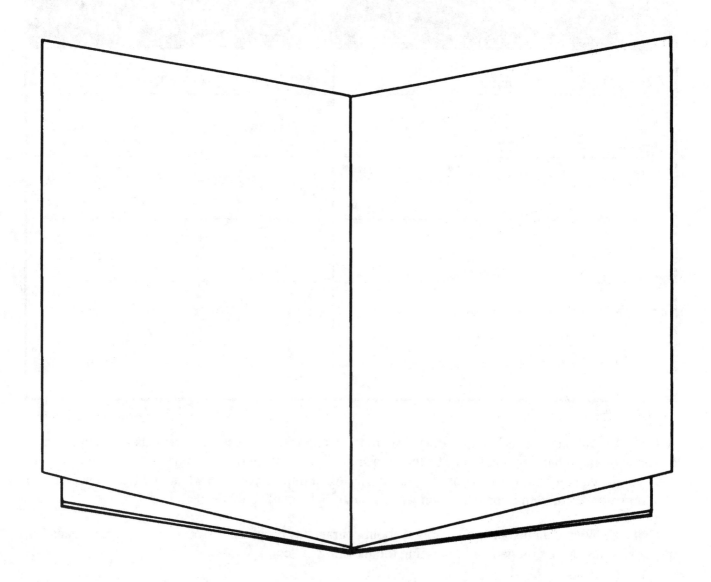

Scientific Explorations

Scientists may also be thought of as explorers in that they dare to go beyond the accepted ways of thinking to discover new frontiers. Often these individuals have been ridiculed and criticized because of their revolutionary ideas. The following scientists have challenged established scientific principles and theories, but their courageous efforts have had results with lasting impact.

Complete the following activity to learn more about these four scientists.

Activity: First, the instructor will assign the name of each scientist to a corner of the classroom. (Placing a sign with the scientists name will facilitate movement.) Next, write on a piece of scrap paper the name of one of the four scientists that he or she would like to meet. Once everyone has made his or her choice, with the scientist's name in hand everyone moves to the corner designated for the particular scientist. (If one group has only one student have that student join another group.)

Step One: After the four groups have been established, visit the library or school learning center and gather information on your chosen scientist.

Step Two: In pairs, write five questions that you would like to ask this scientist if he or she were to visit your classroom.

Step Three: Meet with the other members in your group to compile a final list of questions, adding some and editing others.

Step Four: Now that you know about the contributions that this scientist has made and his or her methods of discovery, answer the questions on your list. Be creative in your responses.

Step Five: Elect one student in your group to play the part of this scientist.

Step Six: Reassemble as a class. Using the list of questions, interview the scientist in front of the entire class.

You may be amazed at what you have discovered!

Underwater Exploration

Explorers not only venture to new and unknown lands, but also into the seas. Without sophisticated technology to explore in deep water, the oceans once held many more mysteries. Not until the 1930's and 1940's did underwater explorers begin to gather information about the world beneath the sea.

In 1934, William Beebe invented an undersea exploratory device called a *bathysphere*. The bathysphere was a round craft in which the diver was lowered into the ocean by a wire rope. A major flaw of the bathysphere, however, was its weight; if the rope securing it to the ship broke, it would sink to the ocean floor. There would be no escape for the unfortunate diver trapped in a fallen bathysphere.

Professor Auguste Piccard refined the design of the bathysphere and called his invention a bathyscaphe. The bathyscaphe was suspended from a large buoyancy tank that had the ability to keep the device afloat. In addition, the bathyscaphe contained a ballast filled with iron pellets that when released by the diver could allow the craft to come to the surface. This safety feature decreased the diver's danger while exploring the undersea world.

Science and technology combined to create modern diving equipment. Early divers carried cylinders of oxygen on their backs and breathed the gas through a mouthpiece connected to the tank with a hose. The tank supplied only two hours worth of oxygen, and only highly skilled divers were able to use the awkward breathing apparatus. Another unfortunate drawback which was discovered was that oxygen used below a certain depth becomes a poisonous gas—carbon monoxide.

In the 1940's, Jacques-Yves Cousteau and Emile Gagnan found a solution to this problem. They invented the Aqualung, or SCUBA™ gear. The Aqualung was filled with a mixture of gases resembling Earth's atmosphere rather than pure oxygen. The gear also provided the diver with this gas mixture at a pressure appropriate for swimming deep below the ocean's surface. This scientific advancement made underwater exploration safer for courageous men and women.

Complete one or more of the following activities to find out more about divers and underwater explorations.

Activity A: Divers have risked their lives in order to gain knowledge about our planet's oceans. Their explorations have revealed alternate energy and food sources. As a class activity, brainstorm the different ways undersea exploration has affected our lives. Use this discussion as a springboard for further research into this fascinating topic.

Activity B: Jacques-Yves Cousteau is a renowned undersea explorer. Research his contributions and their impact on underwater exploration, then write a poem honoring this man.

Activity C: Make a collage of the undersea world as seen through the eyes of a diver by drawing or clipping out pictures from magazines. Attach paper springs to the backs of the creatures to give a 3-D effect to your collage.

Space: The Quest for the Final Frontier

"Seventy-five feet . . . things looking good . . . lights on . . . kicking up some dust. Thirty feet . . . contact light . . . engine stop," said Edward "Buzz" Aldrin as he and Neil Armstrong approached the moon's surface.

"Houston. Tranquility Base here . . . the *Eagle* has landed," Armstrong added as the pair became the first men in history to reach the moon on July 20, 1969 at 4:17 p.m. Eastern Standard Time. The National Aeronautics and Space Administration (NASA), however, had been preparing for this momentous event for a long time. Journey back into the history of space exploration and look at a few of these courageous modern-day adventurers whose work made NASA's visions a reality.

The first man to make any sort of journey into space, and later, to orbit the planet, was Soviet Major Yuri Alekseyevich Gagarin. The first American citizen to explore this frontier was Navy Lieutenant Commander Alan Shepard. Shepard's flight was considered to be a success as the rocket in which he rode, *Mercury-Redstone 2*, blasted 116 miles high above the earth.

As humankind pushed into the vastness of space, a notable mission piloted by Colonel John Glenn was launched. NASA's goal was for Glenn to fly the spacecraft *Friendship 7* in three orbits around the Earth. Within five hours, Glenn witnessed the sun rise and set three times. When his mission was complete, Glenn began his dangerous descent into Earth's atmosphere when the heat shield on the spacecraft loosened. The heat shield was located on the bottom of the space capsule; its function was to protect Glenn from the extreme heat encountered upon re-entry into the atmosphere. If the heat shield had separated from the capsule, Glenn would have burned to death. Fortunately, the heat shield stayed in place, and the capsule carrying Glenn landed safely in the ocean. The courage of these early space navigators was demonstrated once again.

Space: The Quest for the Final Frontier *(cont.)*

As the years passed, NASA commissioned the series of space flights known as Project Gemini. Each of these missions contributed to our knowledge of space, but one outstanding achievement of this mission occurred when astronaut Edward White walked in space for the first time with only a 24' line connecting him to his spacecraft.

Complete one or more of the following activities to learn more about space exploration and space missions.

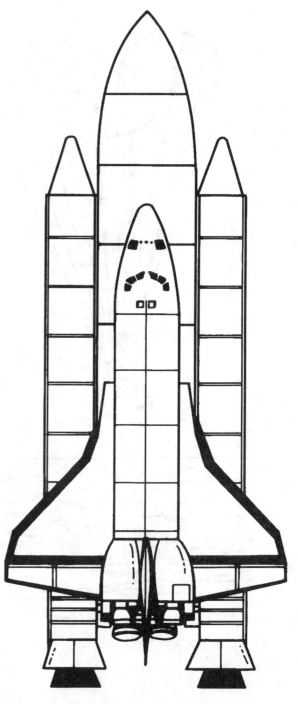

Activity A: Unfortunately, Edward White and fellow astronauts Gus Grissom and Roger Chafee met with disaster when they died in an accident while training for the first *Apollo* flight. In a speech made before Congress, John Glenn spoke of the great dangers associated with space exploration with these words: "Not every flight can come back as successfully as the three we have had so far. There will be failures. There will be sacrifices." Investigate the sacrifice of these three astronauts during this tragic training session and its meaning for us today.

Activity B: Research one of the following space flights and indicate how their missions contributed to the space program.

    A. *Apollo 7* — Wally Shira, Don Eisle, and Walt Cunningham

    B. *Apollo 8* — Frank Borman, Jim Lovelle, and William Anders

    C. *Apollo 9* — Jim McDevit, Dave Scott, and Russell Schweickart

    D. *Apollo 10* — Thomas Stafford, Gene Cernan, and John Young

Activity C: Investigate the details of the *Apollo 11* flight and the three courageous astronauts who flew this mission.

Space: The Quest for the Final Frontier *(cont.)*

Activity D: As Neil Armstrong stepped onto the lunar surface, he uttered the famous words, "This is one small step for man, one giant step for mankind." Make a banner to honor these powerful words. Include pictures, drawings, newspaper clippings, etc., that celebrate America's quest for the last frontier.

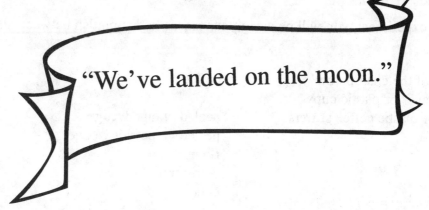

"We've landed on the moon."

Activity E: Working with a partner, imagine and write a dialogue that you think might have taken place between Armstrong and Aldrin as they walked on the moon.

Activity F: What fears do you think surfaced in the mind of Michael Collins as he navigated alone in the spacecraft *Columbia?* Write these thoughts down as if you were Astronaut Collins. Use a journal format to record your thoughts.

Activity G: Obtain information on the current space program. Where do you think the United States' space program is headed as we approach the next century? For example, do you think a space station will ever exist on the moon or another planet?

Science Experiment: Using Your Senses

Scientists must use the power of observation to classify the objects and organisms around them. But while observing the environment, information obtained from the senses can vary significantly. For example, sugar and salt may look alike, but they taste very different. Water and vinegar also appear to be similar but do not smell the same at all!

Choose one of the following activities to learn more about observation and using your senses.

Activity: In this experiment, you will be using your senses to distinguish between similar items.

Materials

a copy of the chart below	coffee	root beer
small paper or plastic cups	tea	cotton
wood or plastic coffee stirrers	peeled orange wedge	wool
water	peeled grapefruit wedge	sand
vinegar	flour	soil
sugar	cornstarch	hair
salt	cola	thread

Procedure

After you and your classmates have gathered together the materials, place a small amount of each in paper or plastic cups. Clearly mark those things that can be tasted with a symbol such as a star and those that should not be tasted with the international "no" sign. To taste samples, use a coffee stirrer; be sure to dip your stirrer into the solution only once. To smell samples, hold the cup about two inches away from your nose and wave your hand over it to direct the scent toward you. (**Warning:** Never taste anything unless you are certain it is harmless and never sniff strong odors at close range, as they can irritate your air passages.)

Record your findings on the chart. For example, "water" and "vinegar" belong under "smell" since this is the sense you used to distinguish them.

SIGHT	SMELL	TOUCH

Sensory Images

We often take our world for granted, neglecting sights, sounds, tastes, and smells that surround us. In *Hatchet,* Brian must use all his senses to survive in the Canadian wilderness. The impressions that Brian's brain receives from sight, sound, taste, smell, and touch are called sensory images.

Choose one of the following activities to discover how sensory images are formed.

Activity A: Reflect on a time when you were alone, perhaps in your house, room, or backyard. You may recall that without the company of other people, you were more aware of your surroundings. For example, did you notice the floors or walls creaking? Were you more aware of shadows cast by familiar objects? Like Brian, you observed these everyday objects and experiences in a new way. Here is a fun way to test your powers of observation. Sit silently in your classroom for two minutes, carefully observing all the sights, smells, and sounds around you. Then record your observations below.

1. _____

2. _____

3. _____

4. _____

5. _____

Share your observations with your classmates and list them on the chalkboard. How were your sensory observations similar or different from those experienced by other students? For example, did the classroom seating arrangement affect anybody's answer?

Activity B: Although our senses allow us to enjoy our world, they are also essential to our survival. For example, hearing the sound of an approaching car or train may save your life, smelling smoke may warn you about the possibility of a fire, and feeling tremors of the ground may indicate the beginning of an earthquake. Think about how being attuned to his environment helped Brian survive. List below five sensory observations he made while he was stranded in the wilderness.

1. _____

2. _____

3. _____

4. _____

5. _____

As a class project, categorize your responses. Upon which of his senses did Brian most heavily depend?

Inventors: Ingenious People of Courage

"Necessity is the mother of invention" (Plato, *Republic*) is a familiar saying that has been realized many times in our history. In fact, while stranded in the wilderness, Brian Robeson makes this observation:

> *Maybe that was how it really happened way back when—some primitive man tried to spear fish and it didn't work and he invented the bow and arrow . . . Discoveries happen because they needed to happen.*

Orville and Wilbur Wright

Many important inventions were inspired by the creative genius of courageous individuals who perceived a need and tried to find a way to fulfill it. Imagine for a moment the ridicule that Wilbur and Orville Wright must have endured when they presented their idea of man in flight. And when Robert Fulton launched the first steamboat, crowds along the shore jeered, calling the odd-looking vessel "Fulton's Folly." If any of these men had lacked the courage to follow their dreams, life would be much different today.

What are your dreams? Do you have the courage to make your dreams a reality? To make a dream a reality, vision and technology (applying the principles of science to improve the quality of human life) must work in tandem.

Here's your chance to dream up something that might improve our world. Complete Activity A first, then complete either Activity B or C, then do activities D, E, and F.

Activity A: Working individually or in pairs, brainstorm ideas that would help humanity. Then select the best idea upon which to base your own invention. Before you begin, however, check the library or learning center to see if your invention is, in fact, original. Once you have done that, follow these steps:

Step 1. Describe in detail how your invention operates and how it would improve the quality of human life. Give your invention a name.

Step 2. List all the materials necessary to construct your invention.

Step 3. Draw a picture or make a model of your invention.

Step 4. Share your invention with your classmates and create a display of all the inventions so that the entire school may see them.

Now it is time to market your invention!

Activity B: Think about how you would sell your invention to the public and design a newspaper or magazine advertisement. Feature both graphics and text in your assignment.

Activity C: Think about the times a billboard has caught your eye. Why? Did vibrant color or special effects on the billboard make an impact on you? Create a catchy billboard to market your invention to the general public.

Inventors: Ingenious People
of Courage *(cont.)*

Activity D: The date is December 17, 1903; the place is Kitty Hawk, North Carolina. You have just been assigned to report a news story on the flight of the first airplane. Write an "eyewitness" account of this historic event. Describe the following details, using reference materials to gather needed facts.

- Who is the pilot?

- What is the structure of the airplane?

- What are the weather conditions?

- What is the length of the flight?

- Describe the landing area.

Activity E: In cooperative learning groups of three, prepare and perform a role play of an interview that might have occurred if you had actually met Wilbur and Orville Wright. List below five questions you would have asked these two courageous inventors.

1. _____
2. _____
3. _____
4. _____
5. _____

Activity F: Draw the airplane that the Wright Brothers flew on that memorable day in Kitty Hawk. How does it differ from the bush plane described in *Hatchet*?

Surviving the Canadian Wilderness

In *Hatchet,* Brian Robeson recalls a piece of advice given to him by his teacher as he struggles to survive in the vast Canadian wilderness:

> ***You are your most valuable asset. Don't forget that. You are the best thing you have.***

But in fact, Brian's courage was tested long before the plane in which he flew crashed and sank into a remote Canadian lake. While still in shock from his parents' recent divorce, Brian had to take his first plane trip without accompaniment by either family or friends. Then Brian witnessed the death of the pilot and, without any previous flying experience, he courageously operated the controls and attempted to land the plane alone.

Complete one of the following activities to discover how Brian was able to face obstacles with courage.

Activity A: Brian easily could have given up, but his teacher's inspirational words gave him the courage to keep going. Look back through *Hatchet* to find and list three other incidents which reflect Brian's perseverance.

1. _____

2. _____

3. _____

Activity B: Positive thinking gives an individual the power to overcome many difficulties and conflicts in life. Sometimes all it takes for inspiration is the repetition of a simple phrase such as, "I can do it!" Recall a phrase or motivational message that has special meaning for you. Perhaps the words came from a teacher, a relative, or a celebrity. Write a paragraph describing how the phrase or motivational message helped you solve a problem or overcome an obstacle. Share your responses with your class.

Activity C: Write your own motivational message. Then, using your best artistic talents, transfer it onto a sheet of construction paper and decorate it appropriately. Create a bulletin board to exhibit all the students' words of wisdom.

94

Creating a "Survival Bag"

In *Hatchet*, Brian Robeson is alone in the wilderness, forced to depend on himself for food, shelter, and survival. Since Brian was unprepared for this challenge, he needed to set aside his fears and meet all problems and difficulties with courage. At the end of *Hatchet*, Brian finally recovers from the sunken plane the emergency kit which holds items necessary both to his survival and his ultimate rescue.

Choose one of the following activities to help you consider what you need in order to survive.

Activity A: Pretend that you found yourself alone in an area such as an island, forest, jungle, etc. You will be there for approximately one week. There will be no outside help, and you will not be allowed to make contact with anyone during your stay. Therefore, communication devices such as telephones and radios, etc., will be of no assistance to you. You alone will be responsible for finding food and shelter. However, you will have two major advantages over Brian: 1) You know in advance that you will be alone, and 2) you will be able to bring along a "survival bag" filled with twenty-five items. The fun—and challenging—part is that the items must all be able to fit inside a large shopping bag that you must be able to lift and carry. Obviously, an item such as a bed will not be allowed. On the chart below, list the twenty-five items you would select and the reason for your selections. Examples include a knife for protection and food preparation or a jug of fresh water for drinking.

1. _____
2. _____
3. _____
4. _____
5. _____
6. _____
7. _____
8. _____
9. _____
10. _____
11. _____
12. _____
13. _____

14. _____
15. _____
16. _____
17. _____
18. _____
19. _____
20. _____
21. _____
22. _____
23. _____
24. _____
25. _____

Activity B: Find someone in your class who selected the same area (city, island, forest, jungle, etc.) as you. Swap your "Survival Bag" lists. Evaluate them to discover how many items you had in common and list them. Then answer the following:

1. After reviewing someone else's "Survival Bag," what new items would you add to your bag?
2. What items, if any, would you eliminate?
3. What items do you believe should be in everyone's survival bag, regardless of the area he or she has selected? Why?

Teacher Information: The Iditarod Sled Dog Race

On the pages that follow is information for your students about Alaska's Iditarod Sled Dog Race. To obtain books and videos about the Iditarod Trail Sled Dog Race, or to order a classroom information packet at a cost of $10.00, contact:

> The Iditarod Trail Sled Dog Race
> P.O. Box 870800
> Wasilla, AK 99687
> Phone: (800)545-MUSH
> FAX: (907)373-6998

Note: The minimum school purchase order is $20.00.

Included in the information packet is background material and addresses for mushers. The packet also includes a history of the Iditarod Trail, information on the checkpoints, statistics on Alaska's Great Race from 1973 on, and more.

Three video cassettes are also available. One is *Beyond Courage,* which is about the care of sled dogs (23 minutes; $12.95). Another video filmed in the interior of Alaska is *Season of the Sled Dog,* which deals with the relationship between musher Mary Shields and her team of sled dogs (60 minutes; $34.95). A third video is *Alaska's Great Race: The Susan Butcher Story*, which highlights the four-time Iditarod winner's life and gives information on what it takes to win (57 minutes; $40.00).

The Iditarod Sled Dog Race

In *Hatchet,* Brian Robeson faces the challenges of nature by chance; however, some individuals face the challenges of nature by choice. One such group of adventureers are women and men who race their sled dogs in the Iditarod Trail Sled Dog Race in Alaska.

Imagine racing a team of sled dogs across a thousand- mile trail in Alaska. You travel day and night in the Alaskan wilderness. You battle sixty-mile-an-hour winds in sub-zero temperatures. When the trail is covered with freshly fallen snow, you search for the four-foot high trail markers with fluorescent orange tops to guide you. You travel along frozen rivers and across treacherous mountains. Sometimes your sled overturns or skids off the trail. Sometimes you or your dogs are injured, or your sled needs repair. Sometimes the ice atop the river breaks, and you or your dogs slip into the icy waters below. You also may encounter hungry wild animals, such as moose or wolves.

Twenty-six checkpoints are stationed along the trail where you may briefly rest. You unharness your dogs and care for your animals. Removing the dog's booties designed to protect their feet, you check their paws for frostbite and other injuries. You feed your racing team and bed them down in a pile of hay or on the boughs of spruce trees before you tend to your own needs. Except for the one required twenty-four hour rest in this race, you might sleep only a few hours each day.

The Iditarod takes about two weeks to complete. Often called "The Last Great Race," the Iditarod Trail begins in Anchorage, then winds northwest until the "mushers" cross the finish line over 1,049 miles away in Nome. (The racers earned the name "mushers" because "mush" was the term early sled dog racers used to signal their dogs to go forward.) This race tests a musher's endurance and self-reliance. In addition, the musher must take proper care of the sled dogs. A musher can be disqualified for failure to do so.

Butcher has been competing in the Iditarod since 1978, but 1985 was probably her toughest year. Butcher was in the lead as she approached the fifth checkpoint, but a moose stepped onto the trail and attacked Butcher's dog team. Two dogs were killed, and several others were mauled in the attack. Although she legally had enough dogs to continue the race (the minimum is seven), she withdrew. Butcher then accompanied her injured dogs to the veterinarian's office in Anchorage, where some of the animals underwent surgery. Butcher returned in 1986 to win first place in the Iditarod.

The Iditarod is a big annual event in Alaska, and thousands of spectators gather in Anchorage for the start of the race. The race is officially organized by the Iditarod Trail Committee, but it takes many volunteers to make it work. Before the race begins, volunteers riding snowmobiles cut and mark the Iditarod Trail and pack the snow. Others work at the checkpoints, signing in the mushers, caring for sick or injured dogs, or inspecting the musher's equipment to see that all the required survival items are carried. Survival items include food for the dogs and the musher, an ax, and an Arctic-weight sleeping bag. Veterinarians examine the dogs at the checkpoints, and radio operators are available to call for help, if needed. The success of the Iditarod depends on its volunteers to work together.

The Iditarod Sled Dog Race *(cont.)*

Both men and women can enter this race, and they are judged by equal standards. Libby Riddles was the first woman to win the Iditarod in 1985. In 1986 another woman, Susan Butcher, won the Iditarod, and then went on to place first in 1987, 1988, and 1990. Only one other person, Rick Swenson, has beaten Butcher's record; as of 1993, Swenson had five wins to Butcher's four.

Choose one of the following activities to learn more about Alaska and the Iditarod.

Activity A: The map of Alaska, below, shows both possible routes of the Iditarod Race. Every year mushers travel from Anchorage to Ophir, but from there the route varies. In even-numbered years, mushers travel north from Ophir to Unalakleet, racing through Cripple, Ruby, Galena, Nulato, and Kaltag. In odd-numbered years, mushers travel a southern route from Ophir to Unalakleet, racing through Iditarod, Shageluk, Anvik, Grayling, Eagle Island, and Kaltag. Every year, however, mushers travel the same route from Unalakleet to Nome, where the race is finished.

Tracing the Iditarod Trail with three colored markers, trace the beginning of the route in one color. Next, trace the southern and northern routes in two separate colors. Label each route. Remember, both routes begin in Anchorage and end in Nome.

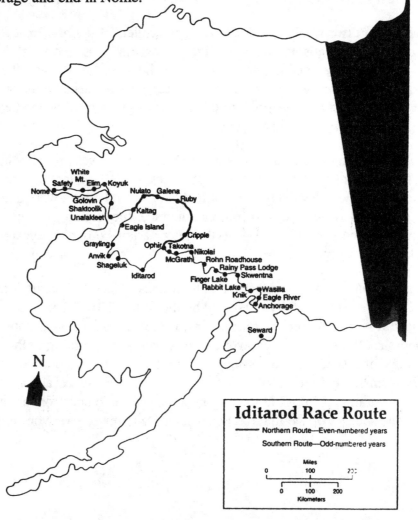

Map reprinted from *Racing the Iditarod Trail* by Ruth Crisman, © 1993. Used by permission of Dillon Press, an imprint of Silver Burdett Press.

The Iditarod Sled Dog Race *(cont.)*

Activity B: Create cooperative learning groups of four to five students. Discuss what you would like to know about the Iditarod and the participating mushers. Then make a list of questions your group will research. For example, perhaps you would like to know how the race originated in Alaska or how the mushers train their dogs, while someone else might want to know what prize is given to the winner. Once you have developed a list of questions, begin your research about the Iditarod. Do not limit your research to just these questions; take notes on any interesting information you find.

The following books may be helpful for your research. You might also investigate newspaper and magazine articles on Susan Butcher or the Iditarod Dog Sled Race.

> Crisman, Ruth. *Racing the Iditarod Trail.* New York: Dillon Press, 1993.
>
> Dolan, Ellen M. *Susan Butcher and the Iditarod Trail.* New York: Walker Publishing Company, Inc., 1993.
>
> Wadsworth, Ginger. *Susan Butcher: Sled Dog Racer.* Minneapolis: Lerner Publications Company, 1994.

For the next part of this activity, discuss the facts your group has discovered under large headings, for example, "Hazards on the Iditarod Trail."

Finally, each student in your group will make five fact cards about the Iditarod, writing them on small index cards. Illustrate your fact cards on separate sheets of paper, then decide together with your group how to display your work. For instance, you can glue all the fact cards and illustrations to a large poster board or put together a group booklet.

The Iditarod Sled Dog Race *(cont.)*

Activity C: Every year, students in Alaska enter a contest in which they design a button to promote the next year's Iditarod Race. Imagine that you attend school in Alaska and design a button to spark interest in next year's Iditarod Race. Draw your design on paper or use whatever materials are available to you. Display your design in your classroom. Use the circles below to help you create your design.

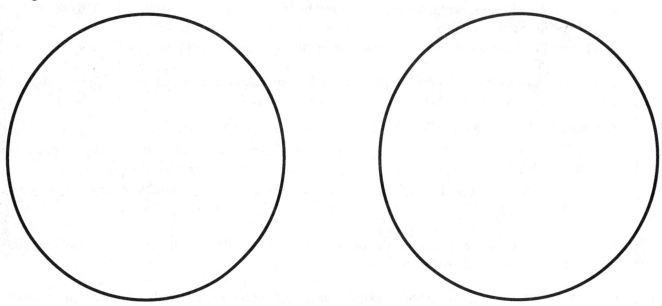

Activity D: After the students form pairs, imagine that one of you is a musher who has just finished the Iditarod while the other is a television reporter for a local television station in Nome, Alaska. Work together to make a list of questions a reporter might ask a musher after the race, then decide how to answer those questions. Be sure to read background information to create an exciting interview. Then rehearse the interview and present it to your classmates as if it were being conducted live immediately following the Iditarod race. Dress in appropriate costumes, if you wish.

The Courage to Change Society:

Roll of Thunder, Hear My Cry

Summary

Roll of Thunder, Hear My Cry is set in Mississippi during the Great Depression of the 1930's. It is the story of the Logans, a strong and determined Black family who, despite overwhelming odds against them, manage to hold onto their 400 acres of farmland. It is the story of their courage in the midst of racial prejudice and injustice. It is also the story of their personal sacrifice, their perseverance, their concern for others, and their belief in their own power to effect their lives.

Mary and David Logan live on the family farm with their four children: Stacey, age 12; Cassie, age 9; Christopher-John, age 7; and Little Man, age 6. Mary teaches seventh grade at the segregated school which her children attend. David works in Louisiana laying railroad track in order to help meet the family's expenses. He returns on weekends whenever he can. Big Ma, David's mother, lives with them and works the farm, helps with the household chores, and cares for her grandchildren.

David asks a friend named Mr. Morrison to remain at his farm to protect his family when racial unrest begins to brew in the community: White men from the Wallace family had deliberately set fire to three Black men. One man dies from his burns; the other two survive but are badly disfigured. Other White "night riders" terrorize Blacks as well, tarring and feathering a Black man over a minor disagreement.

Even though the Wallaces openly laugh about burning the three Black men, their crime goes unpunished. In protest, Mary and her husband organize a boycott of the Wallace store. Mary asks her neighbors to join the boycott and shop in Vicksburg, which many of them do despite the personal hardship this causes them.

The Logans risk losing their land because of the boycott, yet they feel they must do something to demonstrate against this injustice. Harlan Granger, a wealthy White plantation owner, has been trying to acquire the Logan land. Harlan Granger now uses the boycott as an excuse to persuade the bank that holds the Logan mortgage to call in their loan. With help from David's brother, Hammer, the Logans are able to pay off their mortgage and keep their land. However, trouble continues. David is injured by the Wallaces as he, Mr. Morrison, and Stacey return from a shopping trip in Vicksburg.

Cassie and her three brothers also experience prejudice and discrimination as they learn what it means to grow up Black in Mississippi in 1933. The four children and their friends must walk to school each day, while White children ride the bus to an all-White school with better facilities. When the Logan children arrive at school, Little Man is angered to learn that the "new" textbooks they receive are merely the worn-out discards from the neighboring White school.

Indignities mount. In the nearby town of Strawberry, Cassie is forced to leave a store when she protests that the owner makes her wait while he first assists White customers. Outside the store., Cassie is further humiliated by a White girl and her father. When no one defends Cassie, she plots her own revenge for this injustice.

Tension mounts as Stacey's friend, T.J., is framed for robbery and murder by two White boys. The novel comes to a climax when vigilantes drag T.J. from his home in the night, beat him and his family, and attempt to lynch T.J. In order to prevent the lynching, Mr. Logan sets fire to his own cotton fields. All the neighbors, both Black and White, must work to put out the fire. The novel ends with the sheriff and Mr. Jamison, a sympathetic White lawyer, taking T.J. to jail to await his trial. Cassie is then left to absorb the horrible truth of the racial hatred that she has just witnessed. Somehow, despite her tremendous sadness, the reader is left with the impression that Cassie will triumph and succeed with the help of her supportive family.

Making a Chart, Part I

The chart below lists several characters in Chapter 1 of the novel, *Roll of Thunder, Hear My Cry*. As you read the chapter, fill in the chart, briefly describing each character in the space provided.

The Logan Family

Cassie	Stacey	Christopher-John
_____ _____ _____ _____	_____ _____ _____ _____	_____ _____ _____ _____
Little Man	**Mama**	**Papa**
_____ _____ _____ _____	_____ _____ _____ _____	_____ _____ _____ _____
Big Ma	**Uncle Hammer**	
_____ _____ _____ _____	_____ _____ _____ _____	

Other Characters

T.J. Avery	Claude Avery	
_____ _____ _____ _____	_____ _____ _____ _____	
Jeremy Simms	**Lilian Jean Simms**	
_____ _____ _____ _____	_____ _____ _____ _____	

Making a Chart, Part II

The chart below lists several characters in the remaining chapters of the novel, *Roll of Thunder, Hear My Cry*. As you read each chapter, fill in the chart below, briefly describing each character in the space provided.

Mr. Morrison	Mr. Grimes (bus driver)	Mr. Avery
Mr. Sam Tatum	Mr. Harlan Granger	Mr. Sam Berry
Mr. John Berry	Mr. Wade Jamison	Mr. Jim Barnett
Mr. Montier	Mr. Harrison	Mr. Turner
Mr. Lanier	R. W. Simms	Melvin Simms
Kaleb Wallace	Thurston Wallace	Dewberry Wallace

Questions from the Novel, Chapter 1

Directions: After reading Chapter 1, answer the following questions.

1. The Logan farm was once part of the Granger planation. How did the Logans acquire their land?

   _____

   _____

2. Why does Papa leave his family to work on the railroad in Louisiana?

   _____

   _____

3. How do the Logans differ from most of the other families in their community?

   _____

4. Describe both T.J. and Claude Avery. Find an example to illustrate each boy's character.

   _____

5. What news does T.J. give the Logan children as they walk to school?

   _____

6. Consider the school bus incident that occurs as the Logan children walk to school. What does it illustrate?

   _____

   _____

7. Compare and contrast the Jefferson Davis County School with the Great Faith Elementary and Secondary School. Are the schools for Blacks equal to the schools for Whites? Why or why not?

   _____

   _____

8. Why is Little Man angry when Miss Crocker gives him his textbook?

9. How does Mama respond to Miss Crocker when she hears what Little Man and Cassie have done? Do you think that Mama intends to punish Little Man and Cassie? Why or why not?

   _____

   _____

10. How does Mama differ from the other teachers at the Great Faith Elementary and Secondary School?

    _____

    _____

Questions from the Novel, Chapters 2–3

Directions: After reading Chapters 2-3, answer the following questions.

1. Describe Mr. Morrison. What reason does Papa give to explain why Mr. Morrison will be staying with the Logans? Do you think Papa might have another reason? Explain.

   _____

   _____

2. Why is John Henry Berry murdered by drunken white men? Why are the murderers able to brag about their crime without being punished?

   _____

3. Why are the Logan children forbidden to go to the Wallace store?

   _____

4. How does the white bus driver humiliate the Logan children as they walk to school each day? How do the white children on the bus respond?

   _____

5. How do Stacey and the other Logan children get revenge on the bus driver and his passengers? Do you think that the Logans are justified in their action?

   _____

   _____

6. What is the purpose of Mr. Avery's visit to the Logan house?

   _____

7. How do the Logan children react to the conversation they have overheard between Mr. Avery and their parents?

   _____

8. How do the adults in the Logan household protect the children from the "night riders"?

   _____

9. Where is Cassie when the night riders approach the Logan house? Do you think Cassie is brave? Explain.

   _____

   _____

10. Why do you think that the adults in the Logan family never talk about the night riders and the burnings in front of the children? Do you think the adults should speak frankly to their children? Explain why or why not.

    _____

    _____

Questions from the Novel, Chapter 4

Directions: After reading Chapter 4, answer the following questions.

1. Find two examples from this chapter which illustrate T.J.'s character.

_____

_____

_____

2. Why is Mr. Sam Tatum tarred and feathered by the night riders? Why are the Logan children relieved to hear this?

_____

_____

3. Contrast how Cassie and Stacey feel about Mr. Morrison's presence on their farm. How do you explain the difference in their attitudes?

_____

_____

4. Why does Stacey go to the Wallace store? Why do Cassie, Christopher John, and Little Man follow him?

_____

_____

5. Why doesn't Mr. Morrison tell Mrs. Logan that the children are at the Wallace store? Why does Stacey tell his mother the truth? What does this reveal about his character?

_____

_____

6. Find an example to illustrate Harlan Granger's character.

_____

_____

7. How did the Grangers lose the land that now belongs to the Logans?

_____

_____

_____

_____

Questions from the Novel, Chapter 4 *(cont.)*

8. Do you think that Big Ma is courageous? Explain your answer.

   _____

   _____

   _____

9. Why does Mama take her children to visit Sam Berry and his wife? What do you think of her decision to do this?

   _____

   _____

   _____

10. Find an example of Mrs. Logan's courage. Why is her action courageous?

    _____

    _____

    _____

    _____

11. Mrs. Logan and her family have been shopping in Vicksburg rather than at the Wallace store. What does this illustrate about Mrs. Logan's character? Explain your answer.

    _____

    _____

    _____

    _____

12. Explain how white plantation owners like Mr. Montier take advantage of the black sharecroppers.

    _____

    _____

13. Do you think Mr. Turner is courageous? Explain your answer.

    _____

    _____

    _____

    _____

    _____

Questions from the Novel, Chapter 5

Directions: After reading Chapter 5, answer the following questions.

1. When the Logans and T.J. arrive in Strawberry to sell their milk and eggs, where does Cassie suggest they park their wagon? Why does Big Ma park the wagon far away from the market entrance?

   _____

   _____

   _____

2. How does Cassie feel about Mr. Jamison? Why does she feel this way? What does this reveal about Cassie's character?

   _____

   _____

3. What object attracts T.J.'s attention in the Barnett Mercantile? Why does T.J. want this object? How badly does T.J. want it?

   _____

4. How do Cassie and Stacey feel about the handgun?

   _____

5. What do you think accounts for the difference in the way that Cassie and T.J. feel about the gun?

   _____

   _____

6. Describe how Cassie confronts Mr. Barnett in his store. What are the results of her action? Do you think Cassie's action is courageous?

   _____

   _____

7. Outside the store, Stacey tells Cassie that he knows Mr. Barnett was wrong, but Mr. Barnett does not know it, and "that's where the trouble is." What does Stacey mean?

   _____

8. How do Lillian Jean and her father humiliate Cassie?

   _____

   _____

9. How does Jeremy Simms demonstrate courage?

   _____

10. How would you feel if you were Cassie? Do you think that Big Ma is wrong to force Cassie to apologize to Lillian Jean?

   _____

   _____

Questions from the Novel, Chapter 6

Directions: After reading Chapter 6, answer the following questions.

1. Why do you think Hammer buys the same kind of car as the one owned by Harlan Granger?

    _____

    _____

    _____

2. How does Hammer react to Cassie's story about the treatment she received in Strawberry?

    _____

    _____

    _____

3. What do you think Mr. Morrison says to Hammer as they drive away from the Logan farm?

    _____

    _____

    _____

4. What does Mama say to Cassie about the humiliation she faced in Strawberry?

    _____

    _____

    _____

5. How does T.J. react when he sees Stacey's new coat? Why does he react this way?

    _____

    _____

    _____

6. What prevents Hammer from burning down the Wallace store?

    _____

    _____

    _____

7. How does Hammer manage a bit of revenge against the Wallaces? What is Mama's response?

    _____

    _____

    _____

    _____

Questions from the Novel, Chapter 7

Directions: After reading Chapter 7, answer the following questions.

1. Why does Stacey give T.J. his coat? Do you think Hammer is justified in scolding Stacey about the coat? Explain.

   _____

   _____

2. How did Mr. Morrison get the scar on his neck when he was six years old?

   _____

   _____

3. How do the Logans decide to respond to the Wallace's burning of John Berry?

   _____

   _____

4. Find an example of Jeremy's courage.

   _____

   _____

5. Do you agree with Papa that it is not possible for Stacey to have a friendship with Jeremy Simms? Explain your answer.

   _____

   _____

6. Why does Big Ma transfer the ownership of her property to her sons?

   _____

   _____

7. Why does Mr. Jamison offer to back the credit of the 30 families who agree to shop in Vicksburg? How is this an act of courage for Mr. Jamison?

   _____

   _____

8. How will the boycott of the Wallace store hurt Harlan Granger?

   _____

   _____

9. David Logan knows in his heart that he cannot beat the Wallaces or Harlan Granger. Why, then, do he and Mary continue the boycott?

   _____

10. How does Harlan Granger threaten the Logans?

   _____

   _____

Questions from the Novel, Chapters 8-9

Directions: After reading Chapters 8-9, answer the following questions.

1. How does Cassie get revenge on Lillian Jean? Do you think Cassie is justified in her actions?

   _____

   _____

2. Explain how Mama loses her teaching job. Why does Harlan Granger have her fired?

   _____

   _____

   _____

3. How does Harlan Granger learn that Mama was "destroying school property"?

   _____

   _____

4. How do the Logan children react to what T.J. has done?

   _____

5. According to Jeremy Simms, how do R. W. and Melvin treat T.J.? Why do you think T.J. associates with them?

   _____

6. Do you think that Mr. Avery and Mr. Lanier are cowards for dropping out of the boycott? Explain your answer.

   _____

   _____

7. Why isn't Papa angry with Mr. Avery and Mr. Lanier for dropping out of the boycott?

   _____

   _____

8. How is Papa injured on the way home from Vicksburg?

   _____

   _____

9. What injuries do the Wallaces receive during their attack on Papa, Mr. Morrison, and Stacey?

   _____

   _____

10. What do the Logan children fear after seeing Papa and hearing what has happened to him?

   _____

   _____

Questions from the Novel, Chapters 10-11

Directions: After reading Chapters 10-11, answer the following questions.

1. How will the Logans pay their June mortgage payment? Why doesn't Papa tell Hammer that the Wallaces attacked him?

   _____

   _____

   _____

2. What happens when Kaleb Wallace blocks the road with his truck, refusing to let Mr. Morrison pass?

   _____

   _____

3. Contrast the courage of Mr. Morrison with the cowardice of Kaleb Wallace.

   _____

   _____

4. Why doesn't Papa report to the sheriff that the Wallaces attacked him and Mr. Morrison?

   _____

   _____

5. Why does T.J. come to the Great Faith Church revival? How has T.J. changed? How is he still the same?

   _____

   _____

   _____

6. Papa tells Big Ma that the bank has called in their mortgage. What does this mean? Why does it happen?

   _____

   _____

7. How do the Logans get money to repay the bank?

   _____

   _____

8. Why does T.J. come to the Logan's house in the middle of the night?

   _____

   _____

Questions from the Novel, Chapters 10-11 *(cont.)*

9. On the night of the church revival, what happens at the Barnett store in Strawberry?

_____

_____

_____

10. Why does Stacey agree to take T.J. home? What does this reveal about Stacey's character?

_____

_____

11. What happens at the Avery house?

_____

_____

_____

12. How do R. W. and Melvin frame T.J. for the robbery?

_____

_____

_____

13. Find an example of Mr. Jamison's courage.

_____

_____

_____

14. Harlan Granger sends word through the sheriff that he will not tolerate a hanging on his property. Where does Kaleb Wallace suggest they go? Why?

_____

_____

_____

Questions from the Novel, Chapter 12

Directions: After reading chapter 12, answer the following questions.

1. List three possible ways that David Logan might stop the mob from lynching T.J. Evaluate each of these solutions.

_____

_____

2. How do Mary Logan and Big Ma battle the fire?

_____

3. Where is the fire headed?

_____

4. How do Papa and Harlan Granger work together to stop the fire from spreading?

_____

5. How do the townspeople think that the fire began?

_____

6. How does Mr. Jamison once again demonstrate tremendous courage?

_____

_____

7. What motivates Harlan Granger to stop the lynching?

_____

8. Why does Mr. Jamison advise David Logan not to go to Strawberry with the Averys to see about T.J.?

_____

_____

9. What happens to Mr. Barnett? What do you think will happen to T.J.?

_____

_____

10. At the end of the novel, Cassie says, "What had happened to T.J. in the night I did not understand, but I knew that it would not pass. And I cried for those things which had happened in the night and would not pass." Explain Cassie's words.

_____

_____

_____

_____

Comparing Characters

Begin this activity after you have completed your study of the Civil Rights Movement and have finished reading the novel *Roll of Thunder, Hear My Cry*. You may find it helpful to first review the section on Martin Luther King, Jr. on pages 140–144 before you begin this activity.

Think about the fictional character Mary Logan from *Roll of Thunder, Hear My Cry* and the real life person, Martin Luther King, Jr. Although these people lived in different time periods in the South, in some ways they are similar.

Now examine the partially completed chart shown below. Mary Logan and King's names head up the columns. Then similar characteristics are listed in the first column, and examples illustrating this characteristic for each are listed in the second and third columns.

Work with a partner to finish this chart by thinking of at least two more ways in which these two people may be compared.

Characteristics being compared	Specific examples and details of how they are similar	
	Mary Logan	*Martin Luther King, Jr.*
used nonviolence to protest prejudice and discrimination	started the boycott of the Wallace store	helped lead the Montgomery bus boycott
willing to make a personal sacrifice		
had a sense of justice or fairness		

Teacher Information: The Civil Rights Movement in America

Previewing the Material

Before you begin this unit with your students, you may wish to allow two to three weeks to gather materials for the projects on the pages that follow. As you look over the assignments in this unit, you will find teacher information pages at the beginning of each topic. These pages state the materials needed to introduce the assignment, as well as where the materials can be found. They also list books, magazines, and other sources your students can use to research the topics. Some student pages also list resources on a particular topic.

Assess the amount of time you have available to spend on student activities, as well as the type of resources that are available in your school and public libraries. If you are comfortable with an integrated approach to thematic studies, you might use this unit as a starting point, and then let your students' curiosity direct the study; as you will see, the subject of civil rights seems to take on a life of its own once you begin to explore it.

We encourage you to let your students generate and explore their own ideas about civil rights and to give them opportunities to respond personally to what they are learning. If time and resources are limited, you may still use an integrated approach by assigning various topics to different groups of students to research simultaneously.

Teacher Information: The Civil Rights Movement in America *(cont.)*

Sources of Information on the Civil Rights Movement

Here are some sources of general information that you may find helpful.

The Southern Poverty Law Center has a free kit entitled "America's Civil Rights Movement" available for teachers. It contains Sara Bullard's book, *Free at Last: A History of the Civil Rights Movement and Those Who Died in the Struggle,* a video entitled *A Time for Justice,* and a teacher's guide. Copies of this kit have been sent to most middle schools and high schools across the country, but contact the Southern Poverty Law Center for this kit if your school does not already have one. (Note: Your school principal must submit a written request to the Center.) If you have the kit, you can order additional copies of Sara Bullard's book at a minimal cost per copy.

The Southern Poverty Law Center also publishes a free twice-yearly magazine called *Teaching Tolerance.* It contains resources, ideas, and techniques for teachers regarding racial issues and is suitable for grades K-12. If your school is not already receiving this magazine, contact the Southern Poverty Law Center to be placed on their mailing list.

Southern Poverty Law Center
Education Department
400 Washington Avenue
Montgomery, AL 36104
Phone: (205)264-0286

Another excellent resource is the video *Eyes on the Prize,* produced by Blackside, Inc., 1986, in Boston, Massachusetts. This is a six-part video that covers the people and events of the Civil Rights Movement from 1954-1965. Contact your library to see if they have this series available for rental.

Still another source of information that you may contact is the following:

Birmingham Civil Rights Institute
520 16th Street
North Birmingham, AL 35203
Phone: (205) 328-9696

118

Teacher Information: The Civil Rights Movement in America *(cont.)*

Warm-up Activity

Once you are ready to begin the unit, give your students this warm-up activity to help you assess what they already know about the Civil Rights Movement in America.

Activity: Working alone, write down anything you know or think you might know about the American Civil Rights Movement, even if the information is not exactly factual, since the purpose of this activity is to just start you thinking about the topic. Write it on the lines below. Then, share what you have written with a partner. Together, you also may think of other things that you know about the Civil Rights Movement to add to your list. You also can jot down questions that pop up as you share.

_____

_____

_____

_____

_____

_____

_____

_____

_____

_____

When you and your partner have exhausted all of your ideas, repeat the process by sharing your group's ideas with another pair of students. Then, together with your class, discuss and list everything you already know about the Civil Rights Movement in America.

Teacher Information: The Civil Rights Memorial

Maya Lin is the architect who designed the Civil Rights Memorial located in Montgomery, Alabama. The Civil Rights Memorial is a circular black granite tabletop that stands 31" high. On the tabletop are etched the names of forty men, women, and children who were killed during the Civil Rights Movement in America. Lin deliberately designed the table at its low height so that adults and children alike can reach out and touch the names etched in the granite. The memorial is a tribute to the courage of these people and all who participated in this quest for social justice.

Maya Lin

There is also a hole on the tabletop from which water pours slowly over the etched names. On a wall behind the tabletop the following words, taken from the Book of Amos in the Bible, are inscribed:

> *Until Justice Rolls Down Like Water*
> *And Righteousness Like a Mighty Stream*
> **—Martin Luther King, Jr.**

King used this biblical phrase in his famous "I Have a Dream" speech that he gave on August 28, 1963, at the Lincoln Memorial in Washington, D.C. He also used the phrase in a speech that he gave at the beginning of the Montgomery bus boycott in 1955-1956.

Smithsonian magazine has an excellent article about the Civil Rights Memorial, including two detailed photographs, in its September, 1991 edition on pages 32-43. Other articles about this memorial can be found in the sources listed below. It might be helpful to have copies of these articles available to students either in your classroom or school library as they begin to explore this topic.

Boys' Life, April 1991, p. 24

People Weekly, November 20, 1989, p. 78

Time, November 6, 1989, p. 90

Jet, November 20, 1989, p. 4

Southern Living, February, 1991, p. 24

Time, November 20, 1989, p. 69

Lin also designed the Vietnam War Memorial, which is located in Washington, D.C. You can learn about this particular work on page 182 of this book.

Teacher Information: The Civil Rights Memorial *(cont.)*

While examining pictures of the Civil Rights Memorial, students will probably generate interesting questions of their own as a basis for further research. They might ask, for instance, What is written on the memorial? What do these words mean? Why is the memorial circular? Why was it built? Why is there water flowing over the words on the tabletop? What is the connection between the quotation by Martin Luther King, Jr., and the water flowing over the circular tabletop? Gently guide students with their questions if they need help.

For additional information about both the Civil Rights Memorial and the Civil Rights Movement in America, you may wish to contact The Alabama Department of Tourism and Travel at the address and phone number listed below. From them you may be able to obtain a poster of the Civil Rights Memorial, an historic calendar of Alabama, and a Black Heritage Guide that includes a map of the state marked with important historical sites.

The Alabama Department of Tourism and Travel

401 Adams Street

Montgomery, AL 36103

Phone: (205)242-4169

You may also wish to contact the Southern Poverty Law Center, for a free brochure listing all the inscriptions on the Civil Rights Memorial. This is also an easy way in which students can obtain the information needed to complete their time lines on the Civil Rights Memorial (page 124). See page 118 in this unit for the Center's address and phone number.

The Civil Rights Memorial: Journal Exercise

Look closely at photographs of the Civil Rights Memorial, which is located at the Southern Poverty Law Center in Montgomery, Alabama. Maya Lin, the architect who designed this memorial, has said this about her work:

> *I realized that I wanted to create a time line: a chronological*
> *listing of the movement's major events and its individuals'*
> *deaths, which together would show how people's lives*
> *influenced history and how their deaths made things better.*
> *(Smithsonian,* September, 1991, p. 35)

As you look at the photographs, describe what you see in your journal and write down any thoughts, questions, or feelings you may have. When you have finished writing in your journal, first share what you have written with a partner; then, both of you can share your ideas with another pair of students. Be supportive of one another's feelings and ideas as you work together. Next, share the thoughts, feelings, questions, and ideas you have begun exploring in your journal with your entire class.

As a class, discuss the ideas that each group has generated. Each student will then select one or two questions that he or she finds interesting. After creating cooperative learning groups of three to four students, brainstorm ways you can find answers to your questions. Then work together to research these questions. When you are finished, select a representative to report to the rest of the class what your group has learned about the Civil Rights Memorial.

The Civil Rights Memorial: Mapping What You Have Learned

Mapping is a visual method of organizing information. Below is an example of a map in which students listed everything they knew about Martin Luther King, Jr., before they studied the American Civil Rights Movement. Notice that they placed the main topic in the center of the circle. Lines or spokes radiating from this circle contain information about the topic.

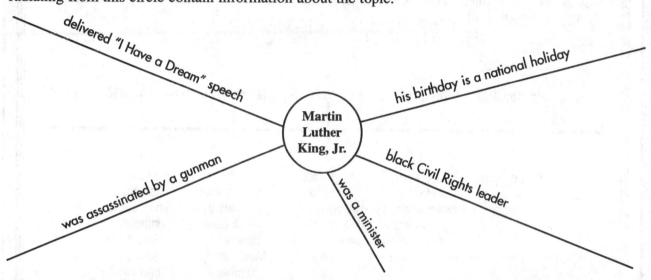

After they had studied the life of Martin Luther King, Jr., students made this map to visually present important information they had discovered about him. Notice the details that are included in this map.

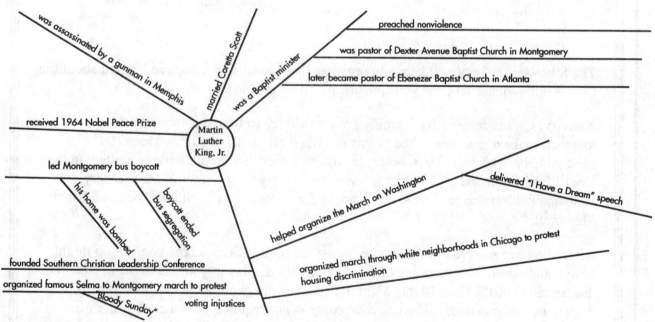

The following activity will help you visually organize the information that you have learned about the Civil Rights Memorial.

Activity: Working with the same partner with whom you worked to first explore the Civil Rights Memorial, make a map of what you have learned about the memorial.

Making a Time Line: The Civil Rights Memorial

A time line shows dates and events listed chronologically, that is, in the order in which they actually happened. Here is an example of a brief time line showing major events in the life of Martin Luther King, Jr.

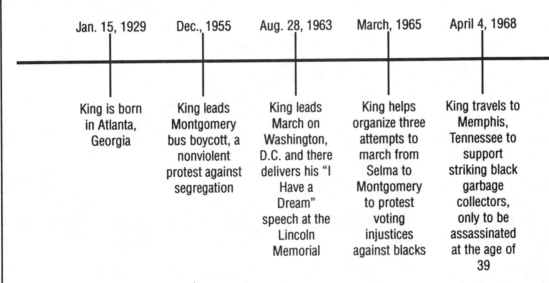

Jan. 15, 1929	Dec., 1955	Aug. 28, 1963	March, 1965	April 4, 1968
King is born in Atlanta, Georgia	King leads Montgomery bus boycott, a nonviolent protest against segregation	King leads March on Washington, D.C. and there delivers his "I Have a Dream" speech at the Lincoln Memorial	King helps organize three attempts to march from Selma to Montgomery to protest voting injustices against blacks	King travels to Memphis, Tennessee to support striking black garbage collectors, only to be assassinated at the age of 39

The following activity will help you organize the information you have learned about the Civil Rights Memorial from your previously completed activities.

Activity: Create cooperative learning groups of three to four students. Working together, make a time line of the events inscribed on the Civil Rights Memorial in Montgomery, Alabama. First, however, you will need to find out what is written on the Civil Rights Memorial. Contact the Southern Poverty Law Center in Mongomery, Alabama (address on page 118 of this book) for a free brochure titled "The Civil Rights Memorial."

After you have received this brochure on the memorial, discuss how your group might design and construct a time line of these events for display in your classroom. Note that the architect of the Civil Rights Memorial, Maya Lin, chose a circular time line to display the information. Likewise, your group is not required to make a linear, or straight, time line—although you may do so if you wish. Be creative as you design, construct, and display your time line.

The Civil Rights Movement: Exploring the Names and Events

Use the map and time line you have created using events from the Civil Rights Memorial as a starting point to develop further questions and discussion on the Civil Rights Movement in America. Select one inscription from the Civil Rights Memorial that you and a partner would like to know more about. It might be any of the inscriptions found on the circular tabletop, or it might be the inscription on the wall behind the tabletop, taken from the Book of Amos in the *Bible* and which reads as follows:

Until Justice Rolls Down Like Waters

And Righteousness Like a Mighty Stream

　　　　　　　　　　—Martin Luther King Jr.

Write a list of questions that you and your partner have about the inscription you selected on the lines below. Research answers to your questions using any resources available to you in your classroom or school or public library. You may even contact the Civil Rights Institute in Birmingham, Alabama, or the Southern Poverty Law Center in Montgomery, Alabama, if you need further information; your teacher can provide you with the addresses. Then work together with your partner to write a brief report on what you have learned.

Responding to What You Have Learned

In addition to your report, find a creative way to respond individually to what you have learned. For example, you might write a poem or personal essay. You could make a drawing, painting, or collage, or use clay to express your feelings with a sculpture. You might even make a model of the person or event you have researched. These are just some possibilities. Be creative. When both you and your partner have finished your report and your creative responses to what you have learned, share them with your classmates.

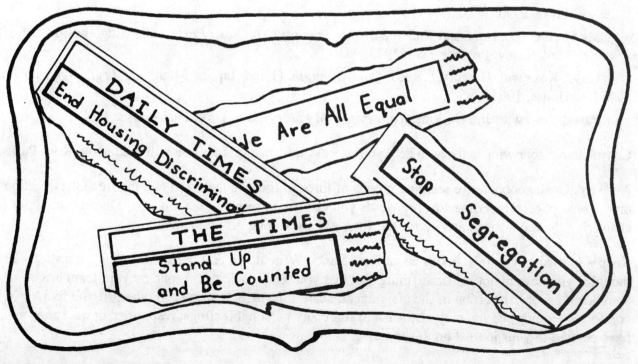

The Civil Rights Movement: Rosa Parks and the Montgomery Bus Boycott

Sometimes the courage of one person can have a tremendous impact on the lives of others. That is what happened when a black woman named Rosa Parks rode the bus home from work in Montgomery, Alabama on December 1, 1955. The courage she displayed on the bus that day and in the days that followed helped launch the Civil Rights Movement.

The books listed below are excellent resources on Rosa Parks. Use these and other materials in your school or public library, as well as books that your teacher may provide, to learn more about Rosa Parks and the effect she had on the Civil Rights Movement.

Celsi, Teresa. *Rosa Parks and the Montgomery Bus Boycott*. Brookfield, Connecticut: Milbrook Press, 1991.

Friese, Kai. *Rosa Parks: The Movement Organizes*. Englewood Cliffs, New Jersey: Silver Burdett Press, 1990.

Meriwether, Louise. *Don't Ride the Bus on Monday: The Rosa Parks Story*. Englewood Cliffs, New Jersey: Prentice-Hall, 1973.

Parks, Rosa with Gregory J. Reed. *Quiet Strength*. Grand Rapids, Michigan: Zondervan Publishing House, 1994.

Parks, Rosa with Jim Haskins. *Rosa Parks: My Story*. New York: Dial Books, 1992.

Complete the following activity to help you process information that you will read about Rosa Parks.

Activity: Create cooperative learning groups of three to four students and together read the questions on the next page. Underline any key words you can use to research the answers. Discuss strategies for answering these questions and divide the work evenly among group members.

Keep a journal as you read books about Rosa Parks. Write down any personal feelings, questions, or thoughts you have about her or anything else that you read. When everyone on your team has completed his or her portion of the assignment, share information with each other. If you feel comfortable doing so, you may also wish to share any personal feelings, responses, or questions you have entered in your journal on this topic.

The Civil Rights Movement: Rosa Parks and the Montgomery Bus Boycott *(cont.)*

1. How would you define the term "segregation"? Besides public transportation, what other public facilities were segregated in the South?

   _____

2. What did Rosa Parks refuse to do as she rode the bus home from work in Montgomery, Alabama, on December 1, 1955? What behavior was Rosa Parks expected to display? What was the immediate consequence of refusing to behave in this way? How do you feel about the treatment Rosa Parks received?

   _____

3. What do the letters NAACP stand for? What is the purpose of this organization?

   _____

4. How was Edgar Daniel Nixon connected with the NAACP? What job did Rosa Parks have in the NAACP?

   _____

5. After Rosa Parks was arrested, what did E. D. Nixon ask her to do? Why do you think she agreed?

   _____

6. How did the courage of Rosa Parks motivate others in Montgomery, Alabama, to protest the unfair treatment of Blacks in the South?

   _____

7. How did those people who wanted to sabotage the boycott fail to threaten and frighten its supporters? How do you feel about these tactics?

   _____

8. Describe the sacrifices that Black people living in Montgomery, Alabama made in order for the boycott to succeed. How long did this boycott last? Explain what the boycott accomplished.

   _____

   _____

   _____

   _____

   _____

   _____

Rosa Parks and the Montgomery Bus Boycott: Creating a Handbill

A handbill is a printed paper listing information about various people, products, or important events. Handbills are of various sizes and are usually passed by hand from one person to another. For example, handbills are often passed out in election years or when important local, state, or federal legislation is being considered in order to inform people about various points of view. The following activity will help you understand the importance of this form of communication.

Activity: Working alone or with a partner, pretend that you are an organizer of the Montgomery bus boycott. Write and design your own handbill urging Negroes (a pre-Civil Rights term for Blacks) to boycott the buses on Monday, December 5, 1955. Be sure to include why you want people to boycott the Montgomery buses.

Use your own words to write the handbill, though they can be based upon actual handbills that were circulated during this period in history. You may also decide what size you want your handbill to be, how to illustrate it, and whether it will be in black and white or color. Be sure that this handbill is done by hand to give it a feel of the times. (Note: Do not use a computer to design and print your handbill. Personal computers were not available in 1955.) When you have finished, display your handbills in your classroom.

Here is an example of a handbill announcing a concert by a church choir.

Come to The Great Faith Choir's
10th Annual Christmas Concert
at The Great Faith Baptist Church
716 South Main Str.
Vicksburg, Mississippi,
on Sunday, December 23rd
at 7:00 P.M.
Admission is free.

Rosa Parks: Writing a Personal Response

The two major political parties in the United States are the Democrats and the Republicans. Every four years each political party holds a convention, meeting to nominate a candidate for President of the United States. The presidential candidate that each party nominates will appear on the next election ballot in November of that year.

Jesse L. Jackson

In 1988, Jesse Jackson, an African American political leader, was one of the Democratic candidates. When he spoke to the delegates, Rosa Parks stood at his side. He introduced her with these words: "Rosa Parks: We all stand on her shoulders."

What do you think Jesse Jackson meant by these words? Do you agree or disagree with Jesse Jackson? Write your response on the lines below, along with any other thoughts, feelings, or questions you may have at this time. Share your response with at least one other classmate.

_____

_____

_____

_____

_____

_____

_____

_____

_____

_____

_____

_____

_____

Teacher Information: The Selma to Montgomery March of 1965

Background

On March 7, 1965, Black people attempted to march from Selma to Montgomery, Alabama, the location of the state capitol, to protest to then-Governor George Wallace that many African Americans were being deprived of their voting rights. Led by Hosea Williams and John Lewis, the protesters began their march at Brown's Chapel Methodist Church in Selma with the knowledge that Governor Wallace had banned the march and had told state troopers to "use whatever force was necessary" to disrupt it. About three-quarters of a mile into their march, the protestors tried to cross the Edmund Pettus Bridge but were met by state troopers armed with whips, clubs, and tear gas that they used with brutal force.

The state troopers' violent tactics shocked the nation. Although the march which began on the day that came to be known as "Bloody Sunday" was temporarily halted, African Americans attempted two more marches from Selma to Montgomery; the third attempt was successful. Spurred by the uncalled-for violence of "Bloody Sunday," President Lyndon Johnson urged Congress to pass the Voting Rights Act, which it did in 1965.

Introducing the Lesson

To introduce this assignment, you may wish to show students photographs of the violence that resulted on "Bloody Sunday." *The Bridge at Selma* is a book for middle school students about this topic; Chapter 3 contains several photographs of this tragic event. You may share this book or other sources of photographs of "Bloody Sunday" with your students.

The Selma to Montgomery March of 1965

Warm-up Activity

Ask each student to pair up with another classmate to examine photographs of "Bloody Sunday." Allow time for them to discuss what they see. Then, have them describe the scenes in the photographs in their journals. Also ask them to write down any personal thoughts and feelings that are evoked as they explore these scenes. When they finish writing, ask them to share their journal entries with their partners.

The books listed below are only three resources that provide information on the Selma to Montgomery March. Encourage students to research these and any other sources of information as they complete the assignment on the following page.

> Garrow, David J. *Protest at Selma: Martin Luther King, Jr., and the Voting Rights Act of 1965.* New Haven, Connecticut: Yale University Press, 1978.
>
> Miller, Marilyn. *The Bridge at Selma.* Silver Burdett, 1985.
>
> Siegel, Beatrice. *Murder on the Highway: The Viola Liuzzo Story.* New York: Four Winds Press, 1993.

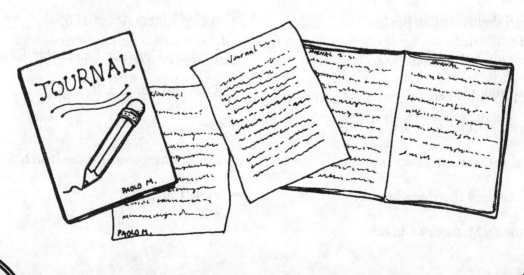

The Selma to Montgomery March of 1965 *(cont.)*

This activity is designed to help you explore another struggle that Blacks living in the South faced—being deprived of their right to vote and participate in our political process. The activity is divided into two parts. In part 1, you will work in teams of three to four students to research the Selma to Montgomery March of 1965, with each team preparing a list of questions and answers based on the information discovered. In part 2, teams will pair off against each other to compete in a question-and-answer tournament about the march. Students will create the tournament rules, a system for keeping score, and a means of determining the winner.

Part 1

As you research the march, gather whatever materials are available to you in your classroom or school or public library. You might also want to contact the Southern Poverty Law Center or the Birmingham Civil Rights Institute for additional information; your instructor can give you addresses and phone numbers. You may even know someone personally who was involved in the Civil Rights Movement whom you can interview for information.

Once your team has gathered its materials, decide how you will share them. Each member will need to read and take notes on important people, events, and places associated with the march to Montgomery. When your team has finished this stage of the project, meet to discuss and evaluate what you have learned, working in pairs to compare notes, ask questions, and review your ideas. You may find that at this point that your team needs to do further research.

Listed below are important words you may wish to include in your research. You might use them as a starting point as you gather information about the Selma to Montgomery March. Feel free to expand upon these ideas and add others.

- Dr. Martin Luther King, Jr.
- The Edmund Pettus Bridge
- "Bloody Sunday"
- Governor George Wallace
- Hosea Williams and John Lewis
- Alabama state troopers
- Mississippi Freedom Summer
- Brown's Methodist Church

- President Lyndon Johnson
- Voting Rights Act of 1965
- Southern Christian Leadership Conference
- Reverend James J. Reeb
- tear gas
- security measures for the march
- Viola Liuzzo*

Murder on the Highway: The Viola Liuzzo Story is an excellent source of information on the murder of Viola Liuzzo. It is written by Beatrice Siegel and published in New York by Four Winds Press, 1993.

The Selma to Montgomery
March of 1965 *(cont.)*

Part 1 *(cont.)*

The questions each team creates should be based on important facts about the march. Do not include obscure questions meant only to stump the other team. Write questions on one side and answers on the other side of index cards. Work in pairs to check the answers to each person's questions. Take notes here for your questions.

Questions	Answers
_____	_____
_____	_____
_____	_____
_____	_____
_____	_____
_____	_____
_____	_____
_____	_____
_____	_____
_____	_____

Part 2

Your team will have to decide which questions are "fair" and which are "unfair" for use in the tournament. You will also need to discuss such things as how many questions you will need. Will each team submit questions for both teams to answer, or will each team prepare only questions to ask the opposing team? As a class, you will need to discuss these and any other guidelines for the tournament. Submit your questions and answers to your teacher for final approval before the tournament.

As a class, decide how you would like to arrange your room for the tournament. Select a student to conduct the question and answer session. You might even wish to include a panel of judges to determine if the answers given are acceptable.

The Road from Selma to Montgomery

The third march to Montgomery began on Sunday, March 21, 1965, with over 3,000 people leaving from Brown's Chapel Methodist Church in Selma. In order to avoid another "Bloody Sunday," President Lyndon Johnson ordered 1,900 members of the Alabama National Guard, along with FBI agents, military police, and U.S. marshals, to protect the marchers, especially through Lowndes County. Eighty percent of that area was Black, yet not one African American was registered to vote. The Ku Klux Klan, a White terrorist organization, used threats, intimidation, and violence to prevent Blacks from registering there. Because marchers familiar with this county feared that snipers might hide in the trees and swamps, helicopters patrolled the woods while soldiers patrolled the highways.

Complete the following activities:

Activity A: Study the two maps. Locate Brown's Chapel and trace the route of the marchers from Brown's Chapel on Sylvan Street along Selma Avenue, Broad Street, the Edmund Pettus Bridge, and, finally, U.S. Route 80 to Montgomery. Also, locate Lowndes County on the map. About how many miles is it from Selma to Montgomery?

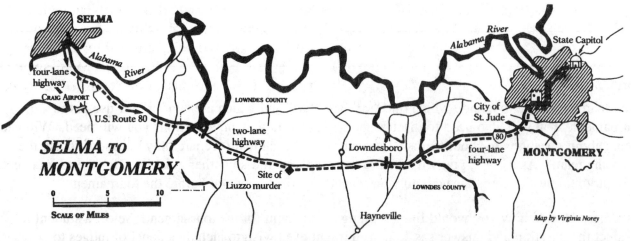

(Maps by Virginia Nourey from *Murder on the Highway: The Viola Luizzo Story* by Beatrice Siegel. Used with permission.)

The Ku Klux Klan

A white robe and hood, a hangman's rope, a cross burning in the night—these are images associated with the Ku Klux Klan, a racist group that thrived (and still thrives) on ignorance and fear. This secret organization flourished in the South in the 1950's and 1960's as Blacks struggled to achieve equal rights.

The Ku Klux Klan began in 1865 in Pulaski, Tennessee just after The Civil War had ended. The Klan started out as a social club, organized by six former soldiers of the Confederate army.

As time passed, however, the organization underwent many changes. By the time of the Civil Rights Movement, the Klan had become a group of vigilantes—people who appoint themselves to keep order and punish crimes even though they have no legal authority to do so.

The Ku Klux Klan used tactics of violence and intimidation to threaten Blacks in the South to "keep them in their place." It was no wonder, then, that in 1960 less than 5% of Blacks old enough to vote in the state of Mississippi were registered. (Seeger and Reiser, *Everybody Says Freedom*, page 160)

Then, in the 1960's, voter registration drives took place to register Black voters in the South. Civil rights workers, many of whom were college students from other parts of the country, went to the South to help with these registration drives.

During that time, the Ku Klux Klan harassed and intimidated civil rights workers, and Klan violence escalated. One day in June, 1964, near Philadelphia, Mississippi, three civil rights workers—James Chaney, Andrew Goodman, and Michael Schwerner—disappeared after being arrested for a traffic violation. Their bodies later were found buried near a dam on a farm near Philadelphia, Mississippi; all three men had been shot. Members of the Ku Klux Klan and the deputy sheriff of Neshoba County in Mississippi were arrested in connection with these murders.

Another victim of Klan violence was Viola Liuzzo, a White civil rights volunteer and mother of five from Detroit, Michigan. She traveled to Alabama in March, 1965, to join Martin Luther King's march from Selma to Montgomery. After this famous march for Black voting rights, Viola Liuzzo drove civil rights workers back to Selma. On her return trip to Montgomery, her car was ambushed by three Ku Klux Klan members who shot and killed her.

The Ku Klux Klan *(cont.)*

In all, more than forty persons associated with the civil rights movement were murdered between 1956 and 1966, and more than 1,000 cases of violence by Klan members and their associates were recorded. Black churches in the South were bombed, Blacks were beaten by White mobs during peaceful protest marches, and Blacks were harassed and intimidated when they tried to register to vote.

Still, it was very difficult to bring Klan members to justice. Sheriffs and other law enforcement officials were often members of the Klan themselves. Members of juries included Klan members, who were sworn to secrecy about their activities. The Ku Klux Klan was a very powerful organization in the South during the 1950's and 1960's.

The following activities are based on information that you have just learned about the Ku Klux Klan. Choose one or more of these activities to help you process this information in different ways.

Activity A: A pie, or circle, graph is a visual aid that can help you understand information that you read. In creating a pie graph, remember that the entire circle represents 100% of something. The circle is then cut into "slices," or parts. Each part of the pie represents a percent of the whole. Here is an example of a pie graph.

Total population of Montgomery, Alabama, in 1954 (Jakoubeck, page 41)
(120,000)

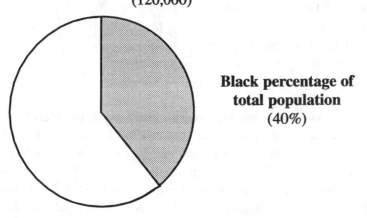

**Black percentage of
total population
(40%)**

Use the pie graph pictured above to calculate the number of Blacks who were living in Montgomery, Alabama, in 1954. To do this calculation, multiply the total population by the percentage of blacks living in Montgomery:

$$120{,}000 \times .40 = \underline{\hspace{3cm}}$$

Then, in the space to the side, create a pie graph that represents the number of Blacks registered to vote in Mississippi in 1960. (see page 135, paragraph form) (Note: Use a compass to draw the graph.)

The Ku Klux Klan *(cont.)*

Activity B: Members of the Ku Klux Klan wore white robes and hoods to hide their identities. What affect do you think wearing masks had on members of the Klan? Try this activity with a small group of students. Each group will design their own mask to be worn by group members. Think about the purpose your mask might serve.

What type of materials could you use to make your mask? When you have finished designing and making the masks, wear them in your classroom. How does it feel to wear the mask? Do you feel different than you did without it? Write an entry in your journal in which you describe your experience with wearing the mask.

Activity C: For this activity, you will need a copy of *Free at Last: A History of the Civil Rights Movement and Those Who Died in the Struggle.* See page 118 for information about this publication. Within this booklet, you will find photographs of some of the people who died in the Civil Rights Movement, including James Chaney, Andrew Goodman, Michael Schwerner, and Viola Liuzzo, all of whom were murdered by the Ku Klux Klan. Cut out their photographs (and, if you wish, the photographs of other people murdered by the Ku Klux Klan) and display them in your classroom. Beneath each photograph include a short paragraph or two about him or her.

Activity D: Create cooperative learning groups of four to five students. The Ku Klux Klan used violence to deal with racial issues. Think of other situations in which a person might be tempted to use violence to accomplish a goal. Brainstorm ways in which the same goal might be accomplished in nonviolent ways. Write down a situation and then list possible nonviolent solutions generated by your group. Evaluate the possible solutions. Which do you think is best? Why? When all groups have finished, have a representative from each group share its ideas with the entire class.

Activity E: Tragically, violence is commonplace in our American society. Have you ever experienced violence in your life? Do you personally know someone who has? In your journal, write about how a violent experience has affected you or someone that you know. If you feel comfortable, share your writing with someone you trust.

Songs of the Civil Rights Movement

"We Shall Overcome" and "We Shall Not Be Moved" are the names of just two songs of protest and determination heard during the Civil Rights Movement. Both songs are based on black gospel hymns that were sung in Southern churches where civil rights workers met and planned events. Singing these songs gave many ordinary people strength to continue the struggle for civil rights. One of these people was Bruce Hartford.

Hartford was a civil rights worker who went to Mississippi after he graduated from college in 1965. In the book *Everybody Says Freedom* by Pete Seeger and Bob Reiser, Hartford describes a march around a square where a mob of white people and Ku Klux Klan leaders gathered to harass the marchers. The Klan leaders then formed a wedge at one section of the square and pushed into the marchers as they walked past. Hartford describes the incredible strength that he and his fellow marchers found in the protest songs they sang during this march:

> *We were singing. Somehow, I can't explain it, through the singing and the sense of our solidarity we made a kind of psychological barrier between us and the mob. Somehow we made such a wall of strength that they couldn't physically push through it to hit us with their sticks. It wasn't visual, but you could almost see our singing and our unity pushing them back. You could see it most clearly when we passed this wedge they made. You could see those Klan leaders trying to push into us. They got within a few feet of us, but they couldn't get closer. By our singing, we actually pressed them back from us, pressed them away from us. Eventually the only way they could get through was to bombard us with rocks.*
>
> *When we started to retreat, and we stopped singing, it was like they had broken our bubble. They moved in on the back of the march and started to beat us up.*[1]

Many of the people involved in the Civil Rights Movement derived their strength from their faith. The Black churches of the South were often gathering places for civil rights meetings, where spirituals became a source of strength. It seems only natural that some of these Black spirituals would be adapted and associated with the Black struggle for equal rights.

Based on a Black hymn titled, "I'll Overcome," "We Shall Overcome" is probably the song most often associated with the Civil Rights Movement. Another song adopted by the Civil Rights Movement is a gospel hymn called "We Shall Not Be Moved." Lyrics from still another black spiritual, "Free at Last," were immortalized in Martin Luther King's "I Have a Dream" speech as he ended with the words, "Free at last! Free at last! Thank God Almighty, we are free at last!"

[1]From *Everybody Says Freedom* by Pete Seeger and Bob Reiser, © 1989
All rights reserved. Used by permission of W. W. Norton & Co., Inc.

Songs of the Civil Rights Movement *(cont.)*

The following activities will acquaint you with some of the protest songs of the civil rights movement.

Activity A: Create cooperative learning groups of 3-4 students to research the following songs associated with the civil rights movement: "We Shall Overcome," "We Shall Not Be Moved," and "Free at Last." Discuss how the song lyrics reflect what was happening in the Civil Rights Movement.

Activity B: Find recordings of these songs in your library using the "phonolog." Look under the category "Pop Titles" as well as "Sacred or Religious Titles" to locate them. Once you find the titles, you will find a list of artists who have recorded them. For example, some of the artists who have recorded "We Shall Overcome" include Pete Seeger; Joan Baez; Peter, Paul, and Mary; and Mahalia Jackson. Make a list of all the artists who have recorded each song. If any of the recordings are available in your library, bring them to class and play them for your classmates. Discuss your classmates' reactions to these songs. (*Songs of Protest and Civil Rights* by Jerry Silverman, New York: Chelsea House Publishers, 1992, is also a good source for songs.)

Activity C: The songs associated with the Civil Rights Movement are especially powerful when sung by many people. Work in small groups to learn one or more of these songs. After rehearsing, have your group teach your entire class to sing the songs together. Listen to how powerful the song becomes as it is sung by many voices. If anyone in your class plays a musical instrument, ask him or her to accompany you as you sing. You might even join hands and sway to the music as you sing. Then discuss with your classmates how you felt as you sang in unison with each other.

Martin Luther King's Dream

Imagine believing in something so strongly that you would be willing to go to jail for it. Martin Luther King, Jr., felt so strongly about the injustice of racial segregation that he was willing to do just that. King believed that people have "a moral responsibility to disobey unjust laws," as well as "a moral responsibility to obey just laws." King wrote these words in his "Letter from Birmingham Jail," where he sat for eight days after his arrest on April 12, 1963, for leading a nonviolent protest march in that city.

King wrote the "Letter from Birmingham City Jail" in response to eight white clergymen in Alabama who urged King not to lead the march. In his letter, King explains why Blacks must stage protests and marches, stating that Blacks can no longer "wait" for white society to treat them fairly, no longer "wait" for violence against Blacks to cease. King's letter to these clergymen has become a famous essay on civil rights.

King was born on January 15, 1929, in Atlanta, Georgia. He grew up during the time of racial segregation in the South. Segregation meant many things—Blacks were not allowed to use the same restroom facilities as Whites, were not allowed to drink from the same water fountains, were prohibited from riding in the fronts of buses, were forced to attend separate schools that were inferior to the schools that White students attended, were excluded from many professions, and were not permitted to eat in most restaurants or sleep in most motels.

King recognized the injustice of this situation. In December of 1955, Blacks in Montgomery, Alabama, began boycotting the buses to protest racial segregation. King was elected president of the Montgomery Improvement Association, the organization which led the boycott. He urged Blacks to refuse to ride the buses in Montgomery, emphasizing that the boycott must be nonviolent. King never forced anyone to participate because he felt that each person must be guided by his or her own conscience to decide whether or not to join the protest.

Martin Luther King's Dream *(cont.)*

On January 30, 1956, two months into the Montgomery bus boycott, King's house was bombed. His wife, Coretta Scott King, was home with their infant daughter, Yolanda, but fortunately no one was hurt. The homes of other Black religious leaders were also bombed during the boycott. Throughout the boycott, however, King continued to urge a non-violent response to the violence directed at them. He also urged Blacks to refrain from hating their oppressors.

King's commitment to nonviolence was based on the life of Mohandas K. Gandhi. Gandhi lived in India during the time it was ruled by Great Britain. He so successfully led the Indians to use nonviolent protest that eventually Great Britain gave up its rule of India. Like Gandhi, Martin Luther King understood the power of nonviolent protest as a means of social change. He wanted to use peaceful protests to help Blacks attain their civil rights.

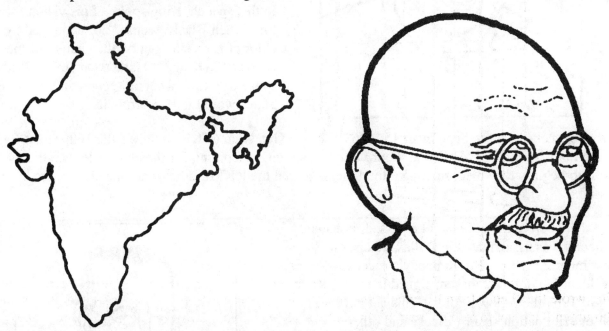

In January, 1957, King was elected president of the Southern Christian Leadership Conference (S.C.L.C.), an organization that influenced the federal government to pass civil rights laws. In the spring of 1963, King and other leaders of the S.C.L.C. planned a march through the streets of Birmingham, Alabama, a city chosen because it was considered the most segregated one in the South. Before this march, King spoke to demonstrators and asked them to march peacefully. But when the march began on April 12, 1963, King was arrested and jailed for leading this nonviolent protest.

Demonstrations continued, and thousands of young people participated in the protests that followed in Birmingham. Police attacked demonstrators with dogs, while fire fighters used high pressure water hoses powerful enough to rip the bark off trees to drive the demonstrators back. Thousands were arrested, many of them children.

Scenes of police brutality in Birmingham were captured by cameras and telecast throughout the nation on the nightly news, shocking viewers. President John F. Kennedy intervened and sent federal officials to Birmingham. Eventually, the city of Birmingham was forced to take steps to end segregation.

Martin Luther King's Dream *(cont.)*

Martin Luther King

In June, 1963, President Kennedy sent a civil rights bill to Congress. To show support for civil rights and to bring national attention to the problem of Black unemployment, a March on Washington was organized. On August 28, 1963, about one-quarter of a million people peacefully marched from the Washington Monument to the Lincoln Memorial in our nation's capital. There on the steps of the Lincoln Memorial, Martin Luther King, Jr., delivered his famous "I Have a Dream" speech. In this speech, King spoke of his vision for a time when Blacks would "not be judged by the color of their skin but by the content of their character" (King, "I Have a Dream"). He also spoke of a time when all people in the United States would live in brotherhood.

But two weeks later, on September 15, 1963, the Ku Klux Klan (KKK) bombed the 16th Street Baptist Church in Birmingham, Alabama. Four young Black girls preparing for the church service that was about to begin were killed, sending a loud message that the KKK did not want the civil rights bill to be passed.

And then, before the bill could be passed, President Kennedy was assassinated in Dallas, Texas, on November 22, 1963. But Kennedy's successor, President Lyndon B. Johnson, signed the Civil Rights Act of 1964 the following July. This act put into law that discrimination against Blacks and other minorities in public places was forbidden. It also guaranteed equal opportunity in employment and education.

Lyndon B. Johnson

Despite the violence directed against him and other Blacks, King did not retaliate. Instead, he continued to focus on nonviolent protest as a means of social change. For his work, King was awarded the Nobel Peace Prize in 1964, a prize which is considered to be one of the highest honors a person can receive.

In 1965, King directed his efforts to securing voting rights for Blacks in Alabama. The culmination of the voting rights campaign was a four-day march from Selma to the state capitol in Montgomery. This march was led by two other civil rights leaders, Hosea Williams and John Lewis. The first time

Martin Luther King's Dream *(cont.)*

that marchers began their four-day walk, they were brutally attacked by state troopers with clubs and tear gas as they crossed the Edmund Pettus Bridge. This violence against the demonstrators occurred on March 7, 1965, and came to be known as "Bloody Sunday." After President Johnson sent U.S. Marshals and the Alabama National Guard to protect demonstrators, King was able to lead the march into Montgomery. The result was that a few months later, on August 6, 1965, President Johnson signed the Voting Rights Act outlawing discrimination against Blacks at the polls.

But the fight for equality was not yet over, and nonviolent methods of protest did not always prevail. Rioting erupted in New York, Philadelphia, Chicago, and Los Angeles over the four years that followed. Then, on April 4, 1968, King was assassinated in Memphis, Tennessee. Although his own life ended with an act of violence, his legacy of civil rights still lives on today.

Choose one of the following activities to help you think about what you have learned about Martin Luther King, Jr.

Activity A: Create small groups of three to four students to research photographs depicting the March on Washington and the march in Birmingham, Alabama led by King. You may come across photos of him sitting in the Birmingham jail as he wrote. Also, look for photos of the protest demonstrations by Birmingham school children following King's arrest. Share the photographs your group has found with your classmates. Then, write a personal response in your journal to what you have seen.

The following books are good resources for photographs:

> Bullard, Sara. *Free at Last: A History of the Civil Rights Movement and Those Who Died in the Struggle.* Montgomery, Alabama: Teaching Tolerance, 1989 (This book may be available in your school library.)
>
> Haskins, Jim. *I Have a Dream.* Brookfield, Connecticut: The Millbrook Press, 1992.
>
> Jakoubek, Roberta. *Martin Luther King, Jr.* New York: Chelsea House Publishers, 1989.

Activity B: Locate a sound or video recording of King's "I Have a Dream" speech. You might check the card catalog under "speeches" or "Martin Luther King" to find this speech. The following two resources contain it:

> "Great Speeches of the Twentieth Century." Santa Monica, California: Rhino World Beat, 1991 (sound recording on compact disc).
>
> "The Speeches Collection: Martin Luther King." Orlando Park, Illinois: MPI Home Video, 1990 (video recording).

Martin Luther King's Dream *(cont.)*

Activity B *(cont.)*

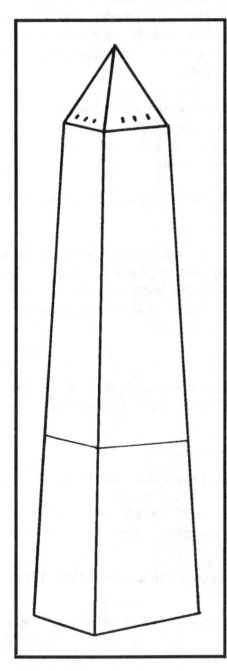

When you have located a recording, prepare to listen to King's speech. Imagine that it is August 28, 1963 and you and your classmates are among the 250,000 people who participated in the March on Washington. You are gathered near the steps of the Lincoln Memorial and are about to hear King's "I Have a Dream" speech. Listen to the speech. Then, write a personal response to King's words in your journal. You might write about your feelings and your thoughts about King's words.

Activity C: King delivered his "I Have a Dream" speech on the steps of the Lincoln Memorial, with the larger-than-life-figure of Abraham Lincoln seated in the background. Imagine that Lincoln's statue had come to life during King's speech. What would Lincoln have said to the crowd of demonstrators after King finished his speech? Work in small groups to discuss possible ideas, then write a short speech that you think Lincoln might have given. Ask a representative from each group to read Lincoln's imaginary speech to the entire class.

Activity D: Work in small groups to make a drawing or model of the March on Washington that displays the Washington Monument, the Reflecting Pool, and the Lincoln Memorial where King gave his famous speech. Research photographs, both of the march and the monuments, from which you can work. Think of a way to represent the 250,000 people who attended this march and gathered to hear King's speech.

Activity E: Work with a partner to research the Nobel Peace Prize. Write a brief report on this topic and present it to your class.

Activity F: There is a famous photograph of Martin Luther King Jr. as he sat in a Birmingham jail in Alabama. Research this photograph by looking in books about Martin Luther King, Jr., or books on the Civil Rights Movement. Study the photograph. Then make your own artwork depicting King in jail for civil disobedience.

Activity G: Work alone or with a partner to research a copy of King's "Letter from Birmingham City Jail." Read the letter silently. Then choose one or two passages from this letter to read aloud to your classmates. Discuss this passage with them.

Activity H: Martin Luther King, Jr. was greatly influenced by Mohandas Gandhi and had a photograph of Gandhi on display in his home. In 1959, King even traveled to India to visit the country where Gandhi lived. Find a photograph of Mohandas K. Gandhi and bring it to class to share with others.

Writing a News Report

Create cooperative learning groups of three to four students, and then pretend that you are all newspaper reporters living at the time of the Civil Rights Movement. Your assignment is to write a news story on any person or event related to civil rights. Remember, a good news story must cover the "5 Ws"—who, what, when, where, and why—as well as "how." Here are some idea possibilities, but you are free to choose any story idea that intrigues you.

- Write a news story about the Montgomery bus boycott.

- Write a news story about King's march in Birmingham, Alabama, on April 12, 1963.

- Write a news story about the March on Washington on August 28, 1963.

- Investigate the lunch counter sit-ins staged by Blacks to protest segregation in the South.

- Investigate the Freedom Riders who rode buses through the South to challenge segregation.

- Write a news story about the first attempted march from Selma to Montgomery on "Bloody Sunday," March 7, 1965.

- Write a news story about the successful march from Selma to Montgomery on March 21, 1965.

- Write a news story about the murder of Viola Liuzzo*, or any other person killed in the Civil Rights Movement.

Discuss how your group will research information and divide the tasks necessary to complete the assignment. Think about how your group will present your news article. You might use a computer to lay out your articles as they would appear in an actual newspaper, although computers for this job were not generally available at that time. Another way to present your news report is to "broadcast" it to your classmates as either a radio or television news program.

*An excellent resource about Viola Liuzzo is listed on page 131.

Mapping the Sites of Important Events

Work with a partner on this activity. Below is a map of the Eastern United State that includes Washington, D. C. (District of Columbia), and the southern states of Tennessee, Alabama, Mississippi, and Georgia.

Use an atlas* or an encyclopedia to write in the location of the following cities and states on the map below. These were the sites of many important events in the Civil Rights movement.

- Birmingham, Alabama
- Montgomery, Alabama
- Selma, Alabama

- Washington, D.C.
- Memphis, Tennessee
- Philadelphia, Mississippi

Next, near each city, briefly list what important event or events occurred there. You many find it helpful to review the information you have learned about the Civil Rights Movement or refer to the time line that you made on page 124. You may identify additional sites on the map below if you wish. When you have finished, display your maps on a bulletin board or elsewhere in your classroom.

Rand McNally Children's Atlas of the United States, Chicago: Rand McNally and Company, 1992, is a good resource.

Jackie Robinson: A Champion Over Injustice

Rookie of the Year! Most Valuable Player! Hall of Fame! These outstanding accomplishments in the sport of baseball are found in the dreams of many players; however, they are reality for only a few. Jackie Robinson was one baseball player who attained all three of these honors. He truly was a baseball superstar, but his greatest achievement was being the first African American to play major league baseball.

Jack Roosevelt Robinson was born in Cairo, Georgia, on January 31, 1919. Because of racial discimination, African Americans were not allowed to participate in major league baseball and were forced to organize their own leagues. While playing for the Kansas Monarchs of the Negro National League, his extraordinary athletic talents were recognized by the Brooklyn Dodgers. In 1947, the Dodgers signed Jackie Robinson to a contract, ending this racial injustice. This courageous athlete led his team to six World Series appearances in ten years. What a victory it was for the world of professional sports and for civil rights! Jackie Robinson died on October 24, 1972, but his legacy lives on.

Complete one of the following activities to find out more about Jackie Robinson.

Activity A: Pretend you have a time machine set for the following: The place is Brooklyn, New York, and the date is 1947. Boom! You have just been transported to Ebbitt's Field, the baseball stadium where Jackie Robinson played his first major league game. Assume the role of fan, teammate, or newscaster. Prepare a list of five questions you would ask Jackie Robinson.

1. _____

2. _____

3. _____

4. _____

5. _____

After writing your questions, answer them as you believe Jackie Robinson would. Keep in mind the tremendous courage he displayed in being the first player to tear down the racial barriers in history.

Activity B: Research the Negro National League in the history of baseball. Look for similarities and differences between the Negro National League and today's major league. Write a brief report on your research.

Baseball: Take a Look at the Stats

Select your favorite Major League baseball team. Using various resources, make a list of all the players on the roster and create a profile of their racial and ethnic backgrounds. You will discover how dramatically times have changed from the days of Jackie Robinson. Calculate the percentage of each racial and ethnic group (African American, Asian, White, American Indian, Hispanic, and others) represented in the team. You will need to know the total number of players on the team in order to calculate the percentage of each racial/ethnic group. To do so, divide the number of players in each racial/ethnic group by the total number of players on the team. Do not forget to multiply your answer by 100 and add the percent sign. Chart your data and summarize it using the bar graph below.

Group	% of Team
African American	
Asian	
Hispanic	
Native American	
White	
Other	

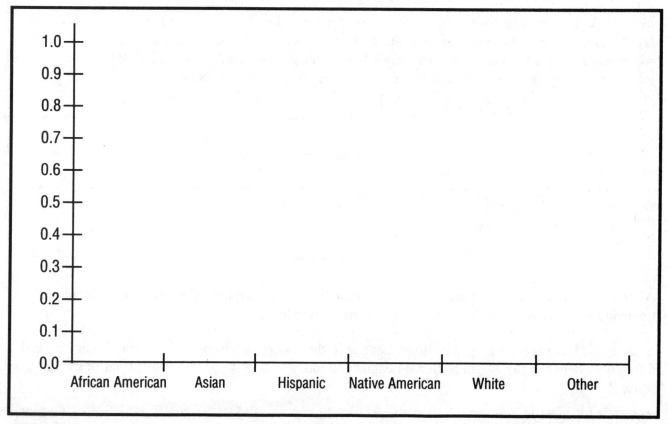

The Courage to Believe:

Shadow of a Bull

Summary

Shadow of a Bull by Maia Wojciechowska is a compelling novel about a twelve-year-old boy's courage to pursue his dream. The boy is Manolo, the only son of legendary bullfighter Juan Olivar, a man who brought glory to the Spanish town of Arcangel with his victories in the ring, but who was tragically gored by a bull when Manolo was only three. Since that tragic day, everyone in Arcangel has held the belief that Manolo would become their next great bullfighter—everyone, that is, but Manolo himself.

Despite his lack of desire to become a bullfighter, a group of *aficionados* (bullfighting enthusiasts) assume the responsibility of teaching Manolo the art of bullfighting and prepare him for the famous annual *tienta* of the Count de la Casa. When Manolo experiences his first bullfight, he is terrorized by what he sees and expresses not only his own fear but his fear for the bull and the other bullfighters.

Manolo's mother is ambivalent. While she deeply regrets her son's fate, she also reminds him of his obligation to the *aficionados* and to the town. With this in mind, Manolo secretly begins practicing his bullfighting techniques with the hope that better skills will help him conquer his fear of the bull.

Ironically, Manolo learns that Juan Garcia, his friend's brother, aspires to be a bullfighter. Because Juan comes from a poor family, however, he does not have the opportunities and advantages Manolo receives as the son of a great bullfighter, and so Juan practices his skills by caping bulls in a pasture. In an effort to gain confidence and courage, Manolo convinces Juan to allow him to accompany him one evening. But after seeing Juan work with the bulls, Manolo understands the *aficion*, or enthusiasm, of a bullfighter.

Then Manolo visits the home of "El Magnifico," a bullfighter gored in the ring. While Manolo watches the doctor who was summoned to tend to the bullfighter's wounds, he realizes that medicine is his true calling in life.

As the day of the *tienta* approaches, Manolo's fears intensify. On the day of the bullfight, the Count de la Casa introduces him to Alfonso Castillo, a much-respected bullfight critic who senses Manolo's reluctance, saying, "Has anyone asked the boy if it was his wish to be here? It seems to me that we have taken upon ourselves God's prerogative, playing with the destiny of a human being." Then he privately offers this bit of advice to Manolo, "Be what you are...in the end it is all between you and God."

Carrying these words with him into the ring, Manolo courageously faces the bull and begins the fight with valor. However, his greatest accomplishment comes when he follows his inner voice and before the conclusion of the fight courageously announces, "I will not fight the brave bull. I am not like my father. I do not want to become a bullfighter." Manolo turns the animal over to Juan, who proves to be a masterful fighter, while Manolo joins the doctor in the spectator seats. The doctor turns to him and confirms what Manolo already knows—that his destiny is to become a great doctor.

Listening to Your Inner Voice

Each of you has an inner voice, though sometimes it may be difficult to hear over the noise of what other people are saying to you. Complete the following activities to help you get in touch with your inner voice.

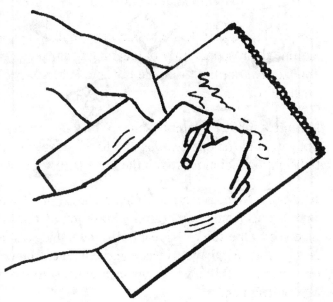

Activity A: Take out your notebook or journal and find a quiet place where there are no distractions. Sit quietly by yourself for a few minutes before you begin to write. When you are ready to begin, pick up your pen and write for ten minutes without stopping. Write down whatever you are thinking about or feeling at this time. Do not pause to correct spelling, grammar, or punctuation. Do not look back at what you have written until your ten minutes are up! Just write whatever comes to mind. This type of writing is called "free writing." It can be about anything, but you might write about a career you would like to have someday. You also might write about something that interests you or about a decision you currently need to make. Try to get in touch with your inner voice as you write.

Activity B: Now do this exercise again, but this time free-write about what other people currently are telling you regarding your life. Are there any people in your life like the six men who tried to interest Manolo in a bullfighting career or like the townspeople of Archangel who had great expectations of Manolo? Think about people such as your parents, grandparents, teachers, or friends whom you believe have certain expectations for you. When you are finished writing, look over your work. Is there a conflict between what you want for yourself and what others want for you? Write about what you have discovered.

Activity C: Complete one of the following to visually express what you have written:

Make a Collage. Cut out pictures and words from magazines and newspapers that express what your inner voice is saying to you. Then cut out pictures and words that represent others' expectations of you. Experiment with different ways of arranging both types of pictures and words on a large piece of cardboard or poster board. For instance, you might place the pictures and words that represent your inner voice in the center of the collage and place the pictures and words that represent voices of others around it. Another way to arrange the conflicting pictures and words might be to place them opposite each other.

Listening to Your Inner Voice *(cont.)*

Arrange a Bulletin Board. Another possibility is to divide your class in half. Half the class will collect pictures, words, and artwork that reflect what their inner voices are saying to them. The other half can display pictures, words, and artwork that reflect the messages we receive from society. Then create two bulletin boards, one for each half of the class. Members of the class display their individual collages on a bulletin board.

Create Your Own Artwork. Create any type of artwork that depicts what your inner voice is saying to you. You might draw or paint a picture of a cartoon; take a photograph; sculpt with clay, soap, or papier mâché; or make a diorama to visually represent whatever your inner voice is saying to you.

Naming Your Fears

In *Shadow of a Bull,* bullfight critic Alfonso Castillo tells Manolo that "Real courage, true bravery is doing things in spite of fear, knowing fear." Former First Lady Eleanor Roosevelt said something very similar in her book *You Learn by Living*: "You must do the thing you think you cannot do."

Both the author Maia Wojciechowska and Eleanor Roosevelt understood fear and its paralyzing effect. However, it is certainly possible to feel fear and act courageously at the same time. The key is not to let your fears stop you from doing what you set out to accomplish.

The following activity will help you explore any fears you have which might make it difficult for you to act courageously. Before you complete this activity, take a few minutes to think about the differences between courage and recklessness, as sometimes people confuse the two. A courageous person is not reckless, impulsive, or irresponsible. On the contrary, a courageous person carefully weighs the risks involved in a given situation, yet acts despite those risks in order to accomplish some greater good.

Activity: On the lines below, list ten things that you would do if you were not afraid. Write whatever pops into your head without stopping to think as you write.

After you have finished making your list, evaluate what you have written. Are any items on your list acts of foolishness? Do any items demonstrate recklessness or irresponsibility rather than courage? Add or delete items as you wish at this time.

Next, rank the items on your list from 1 to 10, with "1" being the least difficult for you to do and "10" being the most difficult. If you are comfortable doing so, share your list with another student or your teacher.

_____

_____

_____

_____

_____

_____

_____

_____

Writing Based on Personal Experience

Complete the following activities to help you explore the connection between having a supportive person in your life and the ability to make a courageous decision.

Activity A: Have you ever encountered someone like Alfonso Castillo in your own life? Has anyone ever helped you make a courageous decision? Write about an important person in your life who inspired you to make a courageous decision. Be sure to include the following information:

- Introduce the person.

- Describe his or her relationship to you.

- Describe the problem you had and how you felt about it before this person helped you.

- Explain how this person's advice helped you solve your own problem or conflict.

- Describe how you felt after the problem had been solved.

Use the lines below to jot down ideas before you begin to write.

_____

_____

_____

_____

_____

Activity B: Now try using art as a medium to express the way you felt before and after you solved the problem that you wrote about in Activity A. You can use paint, photography, clay, chalk, markers, crayons, papier mâché, or any other materials you wish. You could also make a sculpture, a collage, a diorama, or use any other art form with which you are comfortable. You could use two art forms, if you like, one to show how you felt before and one how you felt after you solved your problem. Have fun and be creative with this project!

Conducting an Interview

The people of Arcangel expect Manolo to follow in his famous father's footsteps and become a bullfighter, seemingly sealing Manolo's fate.   But late one night, Manolo walks home from bullfighting practice and realizes that he does not have the same love for bullfighting that Juan Garcia has. Manolo wishes that Juan were his brother, as "then they would not expect him [Manolo] to be like his father, they would have someone else" to follow in Juan Olivar's footsteps.

When Manolo assists the town doctor in attending to a wound El Magnifico received during a bullfight, Manolo begins to think that he might like to become a doctor. He muses that "If only his father had been a doctor, a famous one, a bullfighter's doctor, then they would expect him to be one, too." Despite his youth, Manolo well understands how others expectations of him will influence the choices he makes regarding his own life.

Choose one of the following activities to help you understand the pressures faced by Manolo.

Activity A: Many parents have expectations for their children from the moment of the child's birth, expectations which may be subtly expressed by doing things such as dressing the child in clothing that shows a parent's favorite sports team. Some expectations are expressed in obvious ways, such as choosing a future career for the child.

For this activity, interview three young people and their parents. The three young people should be from different families. You will separately interview each person in the family. Take along a notebook and a pen to record the responses you receive from each person.

Conducting an Interview *(cont.)*

Interview with Parents: Ask each parent to think back to the time of the child's birth. What career, if any, did they hope that their child might one day pursue? What expectations, subtle or obvious, did they have for their child at birth? Have their expectations changed at all as their child has grown? If so, how? Ask the parents to consider why their expectations may have changed.

Interview with Child: What future career do you have in mind? (If the child does not have a specific career in mind, ask what things interest him or her that might possibly lead to a career someday.) What might influence your choice of career?

After the interviews have been completed, make a chart to compare and contrast the answers you have received from the parents and their children. Do the expectations of the parents match those of their child in any of the families? What effects do you think parents' expectations have upon their children? Discuss the results of these interviews with your class.

Activity B: Repeat the previous exercise, but this time interview three adult children and their parents. The parents are to be asked the same questions from the above, but the adult child is to be asked the following: What career or careers did you have in mind as a child? What career do you have today? What do you think influenced your choice of career?

Again, chart the answers you receive. Compare and contrast the answers you receive from both parents and their adult children. Finally, discuss the results of these interviews with your class.

Poetry: Journeying Down Life's Path

In *Shadow of a Bull*, Manolo pursues his dream of becoming a doctor despite the town's pressure to follow in his bullfighter father's footsteps. In other words, he chooses to take another path in life's journey. In "The Road Not Taken," a famous poem by American poet Robert Frost, a traveler faces a similar choice.

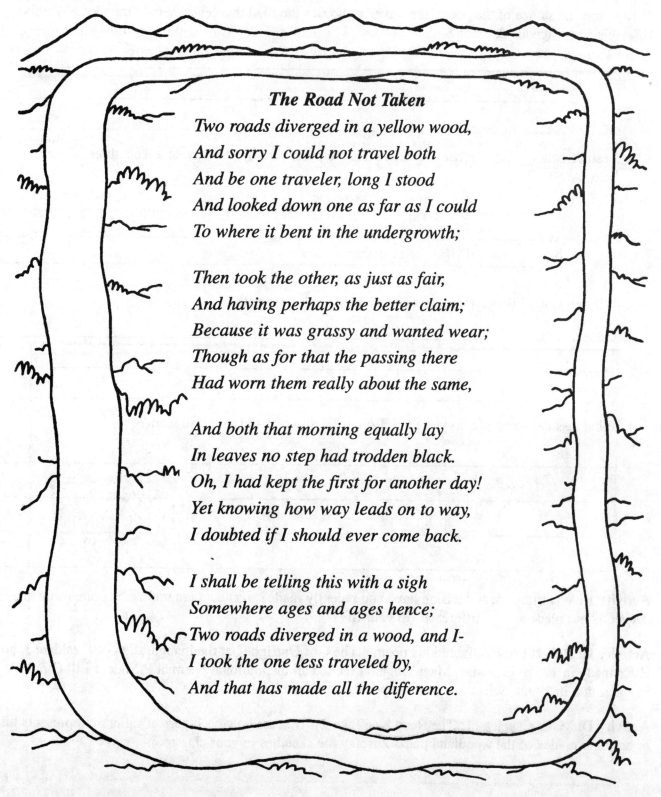

The Road Not Taken

Two roads diverged in a yellow wood,
And sorry I could not travel both
And be one traveler, long I stood
And looked down one as far as I could
To where it bent in the undergrowth;

Then took the other, as just as fair,
And having perhaps the better claim;
Because it was grassy and wanted wear;
Though as for that the passing there
Had worn them really about the same,

And both that morning equally lay
In leaves no step had trodden black.
Oh, I had kept the first for another day!
Yet knowing how way leads on to way,
I doubted if I should ever come back.

I shall be telling this with a sigh
Somewhere ages and ages hence;
Two roads diverged in a wood, and I-
I took the one less traveled by,
And that has made all the difference.

Poetry: Journeying on Life's Path *(cont.)*

Complete one of the following activities to help you better understand this well-known poem.

Activity A: Answer the following questions:

1. In the last stanza of the poem, the traveler chooses the road that fewer people traveled. Why is this a courageous decision?

_____

_____

_____

2. Besides courage, what other characteristics are possessed by this traveler? List three of them below.

    1. _____

    2. _____

    3. _____

3. Why do you think most travelers choose the "well-worn path."

_____

_____

_____

4. What lessons about life do you think Robert Frost wants the reader to learn?

_____

_____

_____

_____

Activity B: What important decision have you recently made? Write a paragraph describing how that decision "has made all the difference" in your life.

Activity C: Robert Frost delivered his poem, "The Gift Outright," at the inauguration of President John F. Kennedy in 1961. Likewise, Maya Angelou recited an inspirational poem at President Bill Clinton's inauguration in 1992. Select one of these poets and research his or her life.

Activity D: Make a sketch of "The Road Not Taken." Discuss how each person's picture represents his or her unique idea of the woodland path. Display the sketches in your classroom.

Courageous Choices

In his poem, "The Road Not Taken" Robert Frost uses a woodland path as a symbol of the choices we make in life. Choosing the best path is not always easy. Often there are many obstacles that can complicate our lives.

One decision young people face today is the choice regarding the use of drugs. Peer pressure frequently leads people down the wrong path. When the traveler in Frost's poem took the less traveled path, he ran the risk of physical injury. He may have also lost his way in the thick growth of the forest. Likewise, making an unpopular decision can cause emotional hardships. If a young person decides not to use drugs, he or she may be ridiculed by peers for not following the crowd. It takes a courageous, determined individual to select the path that is right for him or her, as the traveler does in "The Road Not Taken."

Complete one or more of the following activities to help you think about peer pressure and individual choices concerning drug use.

Activity A: The abuse of drugs and alcohol can cause physical, mental, and emotional harm. Using illegal drugs and alcohol not only affects the user, but also his or her family and friends. Below you will find a list of some commonly abused drugs, including alcohol. Select one and research its harmful effects on the mind and body.

- marijuana   • LSD
- crack   • cocaine
- heroine   • alcohol
- others _____

After this task is complete, compile the information you and your classmates have found into a booklet which can be used as a reference guide for your classroom.

Activity B: Design a banner proclaiming you and your classmates are drug free. Create a drug free statement which reflects your class' position. Each class member should sign the banner as a contract showing your commitment to remain drug-free.

Proud to be
DRUG FREE!

Activity C: Most communities have a drug prevention program sponsored by the local police department. Invite a representative from this program to visit your school to address this issue.

Acrostic Poetry

An acrostic poem takes the letters of a name, title, or motto and uses them to express and reflect something about its meaning. For example, the following is an acrostic representation of the word "poems." Notice how each letter in the word is used to begin a related term that contributes to its meaning.

> **P**ersonification
>
> **O**nomatopoeia
>
> **E**xpression
>
> **M**etaphor
>
> **S**imile

Complete one of the following activities to learn more about acrostics.

Activity A: In *Romeo and Juliet*, by the great playwright William Shakespeare, Juliet asks, "What is in a name? That which we call a rose by any other name would smell as sweet." This often-quoted line suggests that a person's name alone does not tell all about him or her. In acrostic form, describe Manolo and Juan Garcia from the novel *The Shadow of a Bull*, being certain to include their character traits. For example, "M" in the name "Manolo" may suggest the word "maturity."

M _____

A _____

N _____

O _____

L _____

O _____

J _____

U _____

A _____

N _____

G _____

A _____

R _____

C _____

I _____

A _____

Activity B: Create an acrostic using your own name. Transfer your poem to a large sheet of construction paper and decorate it with your favorite colors.

Activity C: Acrostics are used to explain and define abstract concepts as well. Create an acrostic expressing your own personal definition of "courage." You may use names as well as descriptive words to complete the poem; for example, the letter "C" may suggest the name "Columbus."

Writing Another Story Ending

What if Manolo had never encountered a supportive person to help him follow his own inner voice? Create cooperative learning groups of three to four students and brainstorm how the story might have ended differently without this supportive person. Use the lines at the bottom of this page to jot down all possible ideas that come to mind. Then have your group decide which ending you think best fits the story.

You might begin your new conclusion to this novel from the point where Manolo arrives at the Count's ranch for the *tienta*. But wherever you choose to begin, be sure your conclusion is consistent with what the author has already written in earlier chapters.

One way to make your writing interesting is to include dialogue, or conversation, between two or more characters. Here are some things to remember when punctuating dialogue:

- Identify the person who is speaking.

- Begin a new paragraph each time another person speaks.

- Use quotation marks before and after the actual words of the person who is speaking.

Here is an example:

    Jacob asked, "Where are you going this afternoon?"

    "I'm going to meet two of my friends at the skating rink," Garrett replied.

Use the lines below to practice writing dialogue.

_____

_____

_____

_____

_____

_____

_____

_____

_____

_____

Making a Silhouette

Complete one of the following activities to help you understand the pressure Manolo faced regarding his career decision.

Activity A: Create cooperative learning groups of two to three students. Use the dictionary to look up and carefully read all the definitions of the word "shadow." Which definitions might help you understand the title of the novel *Shadow of a Bull*? Jot down those definitions on the lines below.

_____

_____

_____

_____

_____

_____

_____

_____

_____

Think of any expressions you know that include the word "shadow." Do any of them relate to the title of the novel? For instance, how does the expression "To walk in someone's shadow" relate to the title? How does the expression relate to Manolo's life? Record your group's thoughts on the lines below.

Activity B: Ask one of the small groups in your class to volunteer for the following project: Research the type of bull that is used in the sport of bullfighting. What is the approximate size of the bull? Then use a large sheet of black butcher paper or several large sheets of black construction paper taped together to create a silhouette approximately the same size of the bull that a matador faces in the arena. Display the silhouette in your classroom.

Activity C: As a class, discuss how this visual presentation of the bull helps you better understand both the title of the novel and what Manolo may have been feeling throughout most of this story.

Others Who Have Followed Their Inner Voices

Manolo was able to find courage by listening to his "inner voice," guided by Alfonso Castillo, the bullfight critic who helped Manolo make his own decision. Because of Castillo's reputation, Manolo had envisioned "a giant, something more than a man and a little less than a god." When Manolo finally meets Castillo at the *tienta,* Manolo sees Castillo as a wise thinker whose "deep eyes measured up to this vision."

Extraordinary vision or insight into human nature is evident in the lives of other wise thinkers, both past and present. For example, in his play *Hamlet,* William Shakespeare wrote, "To thine own self be true." This line is echoed in Castillo's advice to Manolo. Such wisdom has inspired many of us to resolve conflicts in our lives.

Here are just a few other great people who have possessed extraodinary vision:

Martin Luther King   Mahatma Gandhi   Maya Angelou   Henry David Thoreau

The following activity will acquaint you with one of these insightful individuals.

Activity: Research one of the above individuals and write a brief report. Be sure to include the following:

- Background information about the person's life
- A description of the person's ideas or philosophy of life
- An explanation of how these ideas may be relevant to your life

Use three sources of information for your report. Try to use a variety of resources rather than depending on only the encyclopedia. For instance, you might use biographies, magazine or newspaper articles, or even videos, if they are available to you. You may wish to include one or more visual aids with your report, such as an illustration of the person or a map of where he or she lived.

Accepting a Physical Challenge

"Strike three! You're out!" shouts the umpire. These words are called out again and again when California Angels player Jim Abbott is on the pitcher's mound. While growing up in Flint, Michigan, Jim Abbott's dream was to be a major-league pitcher. He saw his dream become a reality despite the fact that he was born with a special challenge: no right hand.

Jim Abbot

Imagine the courage it requires for any pitcher, let alone one with a physical challenge, to square off against such superstars as Frank Thomas or Ken Griffey, Junior. Yet, it's all in a day's work for Jim Abbott.

In an interview in *Sports Illustrated for Kids*, Jim addressed these fears with the following words:

There are times when you're tired and times when you don't believe in yourself. That's when you have to stick it out and draw on the confidence that you have deep down beneath all the doubts and worries.

Doubts and worries aside, Jim's many accomplishments on and off the field, including a no-hitter against the Cleveland Indians in 1993, have proven him to be a courageous role model for kids everywhere.

Complete the following activities to learn more about the courage required to overcome physical challenges.

Activity A: Wrap and secure cloth around your left or right hand.   Try to play a team sport, such as basketball, tennis, or volleyball, using just one hand. Now try the same physical challenge with an individual activity such as push-ups or sit-ups. (Whatever activity you choose, use caution.) You could also try going through your ordinary daily routine with a physical challenge.

Activity B: Write a short essay describing what your experience of being physically challenged felt like. Include the many different types of emotions you experienced.

Activity C: What lessons can you learn from Jim Abbott's courage? How can his words be applied to your life?

Activity D: Do you know anyone who is physically challenged? If you do, interview him or her about the obstacles he or she must face in everyday life. Be sure to prepare a list of ten questions prior to the interview. If possible, invite this individual to come to your classroom to speak about physical challenges.

Activity E: Although in *Shadow of a Bull* Manolo is not physically handicapped, he is in some ways similar to Jim Abbott in his quest to pursue his dream. Do you think either of these two people believe there is such a thing as an "impossible dream"? Discuss this idea with your classmates.

Teacher Information: Rachel Carson

On the pages that follow is some information about environmentalist Rachel Carson. If you are interested in having your students learn more about Rachel Carson, the following books are good, age-appropriate sources of information on her life and work.

Henrickson, John. *Rachel Carson: The Environmental Movement.* Brookfield, Connecticut: New Directions, The Millbrook Press, 1991.

Krensky, Stephen. *Four Against the Odds: The Struggle to Save Our Environment.* New York: Scholastic, Inc., 1992.*

Latham, Jean Lee. *Rachel Carson: Who Loved the Sea.* New York: Chelsea Juniors, A Division of Chelsea House Publishers, 1991.

Reef, Catherine. *Rachel Carson: The Wonder of Nature.* Frederick, Maryland: Twenty-first Century Books, 1992.

Four Against the Odds contains information on Rachel Carson and three other courageous people who fought to save our environment and the people in it from destruction: John Muir, who saved Yosemite National Park; Lois Gibbs, who revealed the dangers of living in Love Canal, a toxic waste dump where her neighborhood was built; and Chico Mendes, who fought to save the rain forests in Brazil.

Books by Rachel Carson

The books written by Rachel Carson, listed below, reveal her great love and deep appreciation of our natural world. You might obtain copies of these books from your library. You also might read aloud excerpts from one or more of them to your students or make them available for your students to read independently.

Under the Sea Wind. New York: Simon and Schuster, 1941.

The Sea Around Us. New York: Oxford University Press, 1951.

The Edge of the Sea. Boston: Houghton Mifflin, 1955.

Silent Spring. Boston: Houghton Mifflin, 1962.

The Sense of Wonder. New York: Harper and Row, 1965.

Depending on the amount of available time and the interests of your students, they could also research information on the Environmental Protection Agency (E.P.A.), created in 1970, or other non-profit organizations founded to protect the environment, such as Greenpeace.

Rachel Carson's Silent Spring

What if spring came to the countryside one year, but there were no birds singing, no bees pollinating the flowers, no fruit growing on the apple trees, no fish swimming in the rivers and streams, no newborn litters of squealing pigs, no chicks struggling to hatch from their eggs, and no cattle or sheep grazing on the countryside? Where once sounds of spring were celebrated, silence would fill the air, all because an unexplained substance had fallen upon the people and animals, contaminating the countryside.

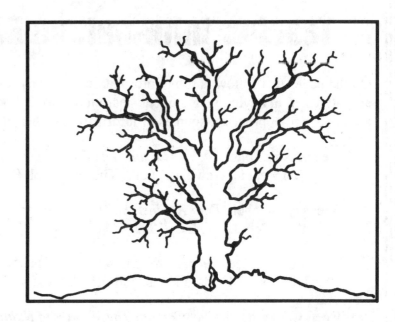

It is just such a scene that Rachel Carson describes in the opening chapter of *Silent Spring,* published in 1962. *Silent Spring* warns of the dangers of misusing pesticides—chemicals used to kill pests such as insects and mosquitoes. At the time this book was published, pesticides were widely used on crops to control insects and had become a huge business for the chemical industry. In 1962, more than $400,000,000 in pesticides were sold. (Krensky, page 41) Despite the widespread use of pesticides, no one was really sure that they were safe to use.

Rachel Carson

Rachel Carson was both a writer and marine biologist. She combined her perspective as a scientist with her great love of nature. She wrote *Silent Spring* to alert Americans to the harmful side effects of pesticides. She argued that pesticides should not be used haphazardly. Rather, they should only be used cautiously with knowledge of the effects they have on the environment and the people in it. In fact, until Carson wrote *Silent Spring,* most Americans were unconcerned about environmental issues.

In particular, Carson questioned the safety of a pesticide called DDT, which was commonly used to control insects that destroyed farmers' crops. She pointed out that DDT killed not just harmful insects, but also helpful ones such as spiders. DDT also killed birds, the natural enemies of insects. Those insects that survived DDT spraying were then able to reproduce unchecked.

Rachel Carson's Silent Spring *(cont.)*

DDT also entered the food chain. Insects that ate DDT were often eaten by small animals, such as birds. Contaminated birds that did not die directly from ingesting DDT were eaten by larger animals which were in turn also contaminated by DDT. Some of these larger animals were eaten by people who had then became ill themselves.

While the concepts she presented are widely accepted today, in 1962 they caused an uproar. The chemical companies and even some people in government attacked Rachel's Carson's conclusions. They claimed that the chemicals were necessary and safe, and that Carson was living in the Dark Ages. They argued that humans should be able to control nature.

Despite these attacks, Rachel Carson held on to her convictions, courageously following her inner voice in spite of much criticism. Soon others began to at least consider her ideas. President John Kennedy was one of these people, and he reacted by appointing a Scientific Advisory Committee to study Carson's ideas. The Advisory Committee concluded that pesticides did, indeed, need to be monitored. The Committee's report credited Rachel Carson with making the public aware of the dangers of pesticides. In 1964, just two years after *Silent Spring* was published, Congress passed a new federal law requiring chemical companies to prove that a pesticide product was safe before it could be sold.

Rachel Carson was a private person. She was a quiet woman who sought no fame, yet today she is known as the founder of the modern environmental movement. She helped others to understand our delicate relationship with nature, and by raising her concerns for the environment and the people living in it, she helped make the world a safer place in which to live.

Silent Spring is a wonderful book that explains the interrelationship between man and nature. Carson points out that people are dependent upon their relationship with the environment. She urged that we find ways to live in harmony with nature.

Rachel Carson's Silent Spring *(cont.)*

Complete one of the following activities to help you learn more about the environment in which we live.

Activity A: Create cooperative learning groups of three to four students. Obtain a copy of *Silent Spring* by Rachel Carson from your library and read Chapter 1, "A Fable for Tomorrow." Then draw pictures or use some other form of artwork to illustrate the scenes described in this chapter. Discuss with your group how you might arrange your artwork and display it in your classroom.

Activity B: Research a food chain. It might be helpful to look in an encyclopedia or in the indexes of books about animals under the topic "ecology." On a large sheet of paper, draw a food chain and label each part. Explain to your classmates how this food chain works.

Activity C: Work with a partner to find the meaning of the phrase "organically grown." Then find out if there are any fruits and vegetables in your local grocery store that are organically grown and list them. Bring to class two fruits or vegetables of the same variety, such as two oranges or two apples, one which is organically grown and the other which is not. Ask four people who do not know which fruit is which to taste the two. Keep a record of the results. Then make a chart comparing the two.

ORGANIC   NOT ORGANIC

Activity D: Rachel Carson pointed out the harmful side effects of misusing pesticides. Scientists have discovered that the overuse of antibiotics can have harmful consequences too. Work with a partner to research newspaper and magazine articles to find out the harmful consequences of overusing antibiotics. Write a report explaining what you have found and present it to your class.

Activity E: Create cooperative learning groups to research a different issue pertaining to the environment. Find out what is being done in connection with this issue to protect the environment. Here are some possible topics, but feel free to brainstorm with your group to choose your own topic, if you wish:

- Nuclear power plants
- Toxic waste
- Destruction of the rainforests
- Destruction of the ozone layer
- Disposing of garbage
- Oil spills in the oceans

Questions from the Novel

After you finish reading *Shadow of a Bull*, discuss the following questions with a partner, then write your answers in the space provided.

1. In this novel, Manolo must find the courage to trust his inner voice in deciding what course his life will take. What is Manolo's inner voice saying to him in the early part of the novel? Find information from the novel to support your answer.

   _____

   _____

2. Think about the people who try to direct the course of Manolo's life. Who are they? What do each of them do or say that may have silenced Manolo's inner voice? Do you think these people have Manolo's best interests in mind? Why or why not?

   _____

   _____

3. Which person in the novel do you think is most helpful to Manolo in finding his inner voice? What does this person say or do that helps Manolo find the courage to travel along his own path? Why do you think this person is able to help Manolo listen to his own inner voice when others are not?

   _____

   _____

4. How do you think Manolo feels both before and after he follows his own inner voice? Explain your answer.

   _____

   _____

5. Would Manolo's decision have been any easier to make if his father had been alive? Find information in the novel to support your opinion.

   _____

   _____

   _____

   _____

   _____

   _____

   _____

   _____

   _____

   _____

The Courage to Fight:

My Brother Sam Is Dead

Summary

My Brother Sam Is Dead is a powerful novel that relates the impact the American Revolution has on the Meeker family. Sam, the eldest son of Eliphalet Meeker and his wife, Susannah, returns to his hometown of Redding, Connecticut, to announce his enlistment in the Patriot Army. Because of the Meekers' loyalty to the English crown, Sam's decision is met with shock and disapproval. Tim, Sam's younger brother, has a mixed reaction to this turn of events, however. It is through Tim's eyes that the reader becomes aware of the profound sacrifices that the Meekers and other colonists make to further the cause of liberty.

The Meeker family earn their livelihood by operating a tavern in Redding, Connecticut, a noted Tory town. In the early chapters of the novel, Tim indicates that despite the fact that Sam had joined the Patriots, the war has little impact upon his family's daily life. In fact, most of the news about the war is communicated through local newspapers such as the *Connecticut Journal*.

As time passes, however, the Meekers and others begin to feel the war's effects, such as shortages of food and provisions. Neighbors become suspicious of each other, questioning everyone's loyalty to the King. When rebel forces sweep through the town confiscating weapons, Eliphalet and the Meekers feel the effects of the war first hand. The war also takes an emotional toll on the Meekers because not knowing Sam's fate causes them great heartache. In addition, Tim questions his allegiance to the English crown as he wonders, "If I went soldier, which army would I join?"

As the novel progresses, Tim witnesses profound changes brought about by the war. Eliphalet is arrested under suspicion of selling cattle to the Redcoats and is imprisoned on a warship. The family later learns that Eliphalet has died from disease, rampant on these vessels. As Tim watches in terror, his neighbors, suspected of contributing to the Patriot cause, are gruesomely slaughtered by the British. Events such as these greatly alter Tim's perceptions of war and hasten his transition into manhood.

In conclusion, *My Brother Sam Is Dead* renders a compelling account of the effect of the horrors of war on the Meekers and other colonists, concluding with the court martial and execution of Sam. In the fictional epilogue written fifty years after the birth of our new nation, the reader discovers that Tim has married and lives a prosperous life in his new country. However, Tim could never forget the tremendous cost of liberty for both his family and fellow citizens and reflects on the war as follows: "But somehow, even fifty years later, I keep thinking that there might have been another way, besides war, to achieve the same end."

The Cost of Liberty

In classrooms all across the United States of America, students and teachers begin the school day by reciting the "Pledge of Allegiance" as a demonstration of loyalty to their country. Reflect on some of the more powerful words of the "Pledge of Allegiance": "One nation under God, indivisible, with liberty and justice for all."

Often, citizens repeat these words without really thinking about their meaning. Our great country was not always free. It was only through the efforts of some brave and courageous individuals— people who fought in the American Revolution—that we have the guarantee of justice and liberty in our land. The novel *My Brother Sam Is Dead* chronicles one family's sacrifices to attain the goal expressed in "The Pledge of Allegiance," that is, "liberty and justice for all."

Complete one or more of the following activities to help you think about the sacrifices made by the Patriots.

Activity A: Tim witnessed the horrors of war first hand when he saw the decapitation of Ned and the execution of Sam. Write a poem dealing with the suffering and hardships of war. Be sure to focus on both the physical and emotional losses.

Activity B: A eulogy is a tribute to a person given after his or her death that is delivered by a close friend or relative at the funeral. Throughout the novel, Tim views his brother Sam as his hero. If Tim were called upon to deliver Sam's eulogy, what would he say? Write this eulogy and read it to your class.

The Cost of Liberty *(cont.)*

Activity C: An epitaph is an inscription engraved on a tombstone. Write epitaphs for the following characters from the novel: Life Meeker, Sam Meeker, Ned, Jerry Sanford. Use the format of "Here Lies___." Draw a tombstone displaying your epithet.

Activity D: *My Brother Sam Is Dead* tells of both the physical and emotional consequences that people endured during the Revolutionary War. Throughout the novel, readers come to understand that the costs of war are great. Some characters sacrifice their lives, while others sacrifice their spirits. The Meeker family is an excellent example of this. Life and Sam die, while Tim and Susannah suffer the emotional trauma of the war. Copy and expand the chart below to illustrate the many sacrifices that the characters made during wartime. An example is provided under each category.

Sacrifices People Endured

Physical	Emotional	Other
experiencing hunger	worrying about loved ones in battle	suffering financially

Revolutionary Ideas

The seeds of discontent with the English rule over the thirteen colonies were planted by Samuel Adams, a man often referred to as the "Father of the Revolution." This man of courage did not fight with muskets or cannons but with words. So began the road to independence; violence was to come later.

Between the years 1765 and 1775, colonists were upset with the unfair treatment and taxation being inflicted upon them by King George III of England. Through his writings, Samuel Adams not only made many colonists aware of these injustices, but took charge of organizing and leading many protests.

One idea he used was that of a "Liberty Tree." This tree, an elm tree located in Boston, Massachusetts, served as a gathering place for colonists to hear speeches and arguments protesting British rule. Sometimes while gathered under the "Liberty Tree," these patriots would hang a dummy from the tree and pretend it was King George III or one of his men. It was also here that some rebel groups, such as "The Sons of Liberty," were born. These groups secretly opposed the British government's taxes on tea, paints, and other goods shipped into the colonies.

Samuel Adams

Although England later tried to pacify the colonists by reducing some of these taxes, Samuel Adams and his pen could not be stopped. Through letters and speeches, Adams influenced many important figures of the American Revolution, including Patrick Henry, Dr. Joseph Warren, John Hancock, and Thomas Jefferson. His inspirational words also incited commoners to become angry about the injustices imposed by the King of England.

Complete one of the following activities to think further about the words which the colonists must have listened to before they began the fight.

Activity A: In the opening of the novel *My Brother Sam Is Dead*, Sam is already committed to the cause of revolution against England. Sam might have been one of the colonists who stood under the "Liberty Tree" and listened to the moving speeches and messages of the patriots. Visualize Sam standing beneath that tree. What types of conversations might he have heard? What kind of speeches might have inspired him to sign on to the patriot cause? Write a speech that might have been delivered by one of these angry colonists. You will need to research some historical facts associated with the unfair treatment imposed by the British on these future Americans.

Activity B: Deliver your speech to the class. Remember that the manner in which you deliver your speech will be as important as the meaning of your words.

A Moonlit Night in 1775

The moon was full and the air was crisp on one historic date in American history—April 18, 1775, the day Paul Revere made his famous ride. Although by profession Revere was a silversmith and an engraver, he is best known for his role as a messenger. Colonists relied on messengers like Revere to receive the latest news regarding important information about the war. Why is Paul Revere considered such a courageous person of the American Revolution? We need to go back in history to find out.

Paul Revere

When Dr. Joseph Warren recruited men to join a group of soldiers who could be ready to fight "on a minute's notice," Paul Revere volunteered. Dr. Warren was a kindhearted medical doctor dedicated to the fight for freedom who gave up his medical practice to organize the soldiers who came to be known as the Minutemen. On April 16, 1775, Dr. Warren commissioned Minuteman Paul Revere to warn Samuel Adams and John Hancock that the British were planning to seize ammunition and firearms in Concord. Dr. Warren also suspected the Redcoats might be after Adams and Hancock as well. As a back-up warning plan, Robert Newman, sexton of Christ Church, was to hang lanterns in the church tower—two if the British approached by sea, one lantern if by land.

Revere's mission began as he and two friends rowed across the Charles River in a skiff, a very dangerous journey because British sentries were on board the English ship, *Somerset*. Slowly and quietly, the three men paddled through the moonlit waters. Upon reaching shore Paul Revere stepped out to find a horse awaiting him. That famous horse had been bred for speed and endurance and was supplied by a wealthy Charlestown patriot. Revere galloped toward the mainland between the Charles and Mystic Rivers in constant fear of ambush by British troops. Indeed, near Cambridge he was pursued by some Redcoats; however, the horse's speed allowed him to elude his captors.

A Moonlit Night in 1775 *(cont.)*

From Medford to Lexington, Massachusetts, Revere began to alert every household by continually shouting his warning of approaching British troops with his famous cry, "The British are coming." It was almost midnight when Revere arrived in Lexington. He went to the home of Reverend Jonas Clark, where Samuel Adams and John Hancock were resting under patriot guard. There were, in fact, warrants issued by the British for their arrest. Revere had accomplished his first mission by warning them of the danger that was ahead.

After completing this phase of the mission, Revere continued riding toward Concord with two other men to alert other patriot soldiers. However, his luck ran out when he was captured. This courageous man of the Revolution did not back down to the British even when held at gunpoint. Instead he defiantly said, "I've alarmed the country all the way up. We'll have five hundred men here soon!" Although the Redcoats attempted to execute him, the sounds of the approaching Minutemen forced them to set Revere free.

Shortly thereafter, the shot was heard at Lexington, which triggered the start of the Revolutionary War and America's fight for independence. The patriots were victorious, due in part to the courageous efforts of Paul Revere. The midnight ride on that crisp, moonlit night in April will forever be remembered in American history.

Complete one of the following activities to learn more about Paul Revere's famous ride.

Activity A: In the opening chapters of *My Brother Sam Is Dead*, Sam enthusiastically relates to his family the historic events at Lexington, and the reader gains insight into how this historic battle affected the townspeople. Paul Revere's message announcing the approach of the British impacted nearly everyone living in Massachusetts at that time. You may wish to reread this section of the novel, and then pretend that you are transported back in time to April 18, 1775. You and your family own a farmhouse located on the route that Paul Revere traveled as he sounded his famous message: "The British are coming!" What would your diary entry for that night look like? What fears might have entered your thoughts? Bear in mind that the British were a mighty enemy.

A Moonlit Night in 1775 *(cont.)*

Activity B: Sam Meeker voluntarily joins the colonists' army in their fight for freedom. In chapter 1, he valiantly recounts the battle at Lexington and Concord and is very proud to be a soldier for the Patriots. Pretend that you are Sam and that you meet a friend who is unsure of his position regarding the side he favors in the Revolution. How would you try to convince him to join the colonists' cause? Work with a partner to write a dialogue that might have taken place between the two of you; then, role play this conversation in front of your classmates.

Activity C: The Revolutionary War was an event that led to the birth of our nation. Since then, the United States has fought in several other wars, such as the Civil War, World Wars I and II, the Vietnam War, and the Gulf War. Although warfare has dramatically changed over the centuries, one thing remains constant: the courage of the soldiers, the men and women who fought for freedom. Fill in the chart below with information about each war. Some categories may require more than one response. If you cannot find any information pertaining to a certain category, write the word "none."

	Land weapons	Sea weapons	Air weapons
Revolution			
Civil War			
World War I			
World War II			
Vietnam			
Gulf War			

The Courage of Thomas Paine

Although Samuel Adams was responsible for sparking the Revolution, pamphlet writer and newspaper editor Thomas Paine kept the flames of liberty alive through his writing. His words echoed throughout the colonies as a constant source of inspiration. His famous pamphlet, "The Crisis," began with such thought-provoking ideas as, "These are the times that try men's souls...Tyranny, like hell, is not easily conquered; yet we have this consolation with us, that the harder the conflict, the more glorious the triumph."

General George Washington read Paine's message to his troops before they attempted the historic crossing of the Delaware River on Christmas night. Paine's words helped these brave men face the hazardous conditions of the winter storm as well as the horrors of the battle that awaited them upon their arrival in Trenton.

Complete one of the following activities to learn more about Thomas Paine.

Activity A: Thomas Paine was the editor of the *Pennsylvania Journal,* a newspaper which supported the Patriots' cause. Work in cooperative learning groups of four to five students to design the front page of the *Pennsylvania Journal* with the date of December 26, 1765. Base your design on the layout of a real newspaper. Include articles, advertisements, and headlines in your newspaper. Place your work in columns.

In Chapter 3 of *My Brother Sam Is Dead,* Tim indicates that his knowledge of the war was gained through reading the *Connecticut Journal.* However, Tim also reveals that his father brought home a copy of Rivington's *Gazette* from Verplanck. This newspaper promoted the Tory point of view. As an option to the above exercise, create your own version of the Tory newspaper. Remember to make your opinion favor British control of the colonies.

Activity B: People today continue to hold conflicting points of view on many issues. Write an essay which will persuade others to adopt your position on a particular issue. Some ideas for topics include capital punishment, euthanasia or mercy killing, animal testing for scientific research, keeping animals in captivity, or smoking in public places. Brainstorm other writing topics with your class.

Activity C: Research the historic crossing of the Delaware by General Washington and his troops during the Revolutionary War. Assume the identity of either General Washington or one of his soldiers; then write a letter to a loved one, expressing some thoughts you may have had before this critical battle.

Art Activity: Tory v. Colonist

Not only did the British and the Patriots have opposing viewpoints on the issue of American independence, their armies were very different. The British soldiers were supplied with enough food, artillery, and other provisions throughout the course of the war, while the Patriot soldiers were often hungry, carried makeshift weapons, and lacked other basic necessities.

Another significant difference was the type of uniform each side wore. Throughout the novel *My Brother Sam Is Dead*, the Collier brothers describe the clothing associated with the soldiers on each side. In the space below, draw a picture illustrating the two types of uniforms worn in the Revolutionary War—but do not research this assignment. Instead, draw your pictures from the mental images and impressions you received while reading the novel.

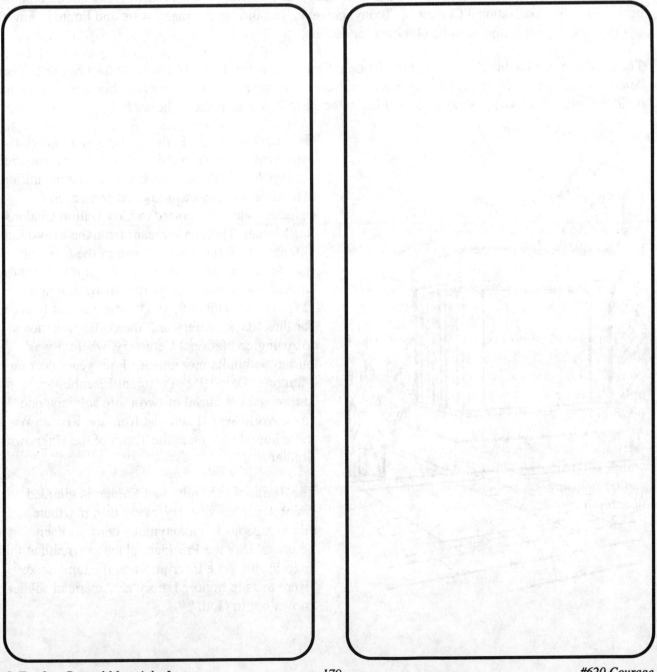

War Memorials

Sam Meeker was only one of many soldiers who died for the cause of liberty during the American Revolution. Since the time of the Revolutionary War, the United States has lost countless numbers of courageous men and women to battle. Unfortunately, if we page through our history books, we discover Tim's final wish in *My Brother Sam Is Dead*—". . . that there might have been another way, besides war, to achieve the same end"—has not yet become a reality. In fact, our government's involvement in war has cost a tremendous number of lives since its first struggle for freedom.

Perhaps the best reminder of war's devastation and destruction is Arlington National Cemetery in Arlington, Virginia. When visitors go to this cemetery, silence falls over them when they view the seemingly endless sea of grave markers for generals, astronauts, and Presidents, as well as those for the common soldier, all heroes in their own right. Initially, any soldier who served with honor could be buried in Arlington National Cemetery. Today, however, because of the many wars and limited number of grave sites, permission must be obtained for burials.

The most famous landmark in Arlington National Cemetery is the Tomb of the Unknown Soldier. The "unknown soldier" buried there represents all soldiers who gave their lives in battle but were unable to be identified. How was this particular soldier selected to hold this place of honor?

The story begins in France, where there are four American cemeteries filled with soldiers who died during World War I. One body of an unidentified American soldier was removed from each cemetery and transported to City Hall in Chalons-sur-Marne. There, a sergeant from the Fifty-ninth Infantry randomly selected one of the four coffins and put a bouquet of White roses on it. The coffin of this soldier was transported to Washington, D.C., on November 9, 1954, where it was honored for three days. Afterword, the coffin was moved to Arlington National Cemetery, where it was buried within its monument. Four years later on Memorial Day, 1958, President Eisenhower authorized the burial of two more soldiers, one from World War II and one from the Korean War, to be buried alongside the Tomb of the Unknown Soldier.

The Tomb of the Unknown Soldier is guarded twenty-four hours a day, every day, in tribute to all courageous but anonymous heroes. Each Veterans' Day the President places a wreath at this historic site. The inscription on the tomb reads, "Here rests in honored glory an American soldier known but to God."

War Memorials *(cont.)*

Complete one of the following activities to learn more about Arlington National Cemetery as well as events that honor our veteran soldiers.

Activity A: One grave in Arlington National Cemetery is marked with an eternal flame. This is the final resting spot of President John F. Kennedy. The eternal flame symbolizes a line from Kennedy's inaugural address, "The energy, the faith, the devotion which we bring to this endeavor will light our country and all who serve it, and the glow from that fire can truly light the world."

Research the names of other members of the Kennedy family buried along with President Kennedy. List any other important historical figures who are also buried at Arlington National Cemetery.

Activity B: Veterans' Day is just one patriotic holiday on which we remember the soldiers who fought and returned from war. Another is Memorial Day, the day we honor the brave individuals who died defending our country. Many of us know at least one veteran of a past war. Interview him or her regarding his or her war experiences. Prior to your interview, prepare a list of ten questions you wish to ask your subject. For example, you may ask this veteran to relate his or her most courageous experience.

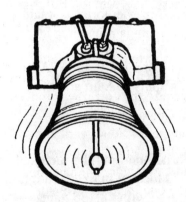

Activity C: Fireworks! Parades! Picnics! Everything is red, white, and blue. There's no doubt about it; it's the Fourth of July, or Independence Day. This holiday celebrates the freedom that was gained through the sacrifices of our Revolutionary War heroes. Church bells ring throughout our land in commemoration of the Liberty Bell which originally rang to proclaim our independence from England.

Travel back through time to Mount Vernon, the home of President George Washington. George and Martha have hired you to organize the first Independence Day celebration. Here's your task:

1. Draw up a list of guests. Include five people from the Revolutionary period and five people from the present. Explain why you invited these specific people.

2. What type of food and beverage would you serve? Would you treat the Colonial people to a sampling or our present-day foods or would you serve foods typical of their period?

3. Would there be a dress code for this important event?

4. What type of entertainment would you provide? Make sure your music, games, etc., appeal to guests of both time periods.

5. Design an invitation to the Washington Independence Day party.

War Memorials *(cont.)*

The Iwo Jima Memorial

Iwo Jima is an island located in the northwest part of the Pacific Ocean. During World War II, in March, 1945, 5,000 courageous men of the Third, Fourth, and Fifth Marine Divisions sacrificed their lives to capture this island from the Japanese. The United States needed to overtake this strategic island because the Japanese fighter planes attacked American bombers from this location during World War II.

"Iwo Jima"

Just outside of Arlington National Cemetery, overlooking the Potomac River, stands a bronze statue of Ira H. Hayes and his fellow Marines. These soldiers are proudly raising the flag on Mt. Suribacki on the island of Iwo Jima, signifying the American victory. This famous memorial was inspired by a Pulitzer Prize-winning photograph by Joe Rosenthal. The statue is a testimonial to all the brave men who fought valiantly for their country.

Complete the following activity to learn more about this statue.

Activity: The official name of the Iwo Jima statue is the U.S. Marine Corps War Memorial. Obtain a picture of this famous war memorial and write a paragraph explaining what feelings it inspires in you.

The inscription on the base of this memorial reads, "Uncommon valor was a common virtue." As a class, discuss the meaning of this inscription. How do these timeless words apply to Sam and the soldiers of the American Revolution?

The Vietnam Veterans' Memorial

On Veterans' Day, November 11, 1984, our country dedicated a new memorial honoring the men and women who fought in the Vietnam War. The Vietnam Veterans' Memorial is located in Constitution Gardens, Washington, D.C. Its simple design—a low shiny black wall covered with 58,156 names—makes a powerful statement. Visitors are deeply moved by the tremendous loss of life reflected in this memorial.

The Vietnam War was a bitter struggle for Americans abroad and on the home front in the late 1960's and early 1970's. The United States was aiding the South Vietnamese in their fight to remain free from the North Vietnam, a Communist government. Opinion was divided concerning America's involvement in this conflict. Consequently, many Americans exercised their rights to free speech by protesting the war with marches and demonstrations. In addition, the horrors of the war came into every family's living room through nightly newscasts; Americans received a firsthand account of the bloody battlefields thousands of miles away. Contrast this with the Revolutionary War, when the Meekers had little news of Sam and his war activities.

War Memorials (cont.)

Complete one of the following activities to find out more about the Vietnam War.

Activity A: Some colonists supported the Patriots in the Revolutionary War, and members of the Patriot Army are glorified in American history books. On the other hand, because of people's divided opinions on the Vietnam War, returning soldiers did not receive the honor and respect due to them. Write a letter to a Vietnam War veteran or a family member of a deceased veteran, thanking him or her for valiant participation. Letters may be sent to your local Veterans Association.

Activity B: For "service above and beyond the call of duty," many soldiers receive decorations and medals of honor. In 1782, George Washington established the first U.S. military decoration, the Badge of Military Merit. Only three soldiers were awarded this honor by Washington. In 1932, this medal became known as the Purple Heart, which is given to soldiers who have been injured in battle. The Purple Heart is also awarded to soldiers posthumously, or after their death, in which case medals are given to the soldiers' families.

During the Civil War, Congress approved the Medal of Honor, known today as the Congressional Medal of Honor. It is our government's highest military award.

Write an essay on the following topic: If you were General Washington, to whom would you present the Badge of Military Merit? Give reasons for your selections. In your writing, address the following question: Do you think Sam Meeker should receive this award? Give reasons for your answer.

Activity C: Research the design of the Purple Heart or Congressional Medal of Honor and sketch it on a sheet of paper.

Let Freedom Ring

The Liberty Bell is a well-known symbol of the freedom attained by the courageous colonists in the early history of our country. This famous bell was rung on July 8, 1776, to honor the signing of the Declaration of Independence. The words inscribed on the Liberty Bell, "Proclaim liberty throughout all the land unto all inhabitants thereof," is a quote from the Bible. All visitors to the Tower Room of Independence Hall in Philadelphia, Pennsylvania are able to view this symbol of our nation's pride. The bell is no longer regularly rung due to its obvious crack, but it is still struck on such special occasions as the Bicentennial Celebration in 1976.

Complete the following activity to learn more about the Liberty Bell.

Activity: Below you will find a half-completed picture of the Liberty Bell. Finish the drawing using your artistic talents and the mathematical property of symmetry, or the concept of a mirror image— what appears on one side of a figure appears on the other side, (except for the crack) as well.

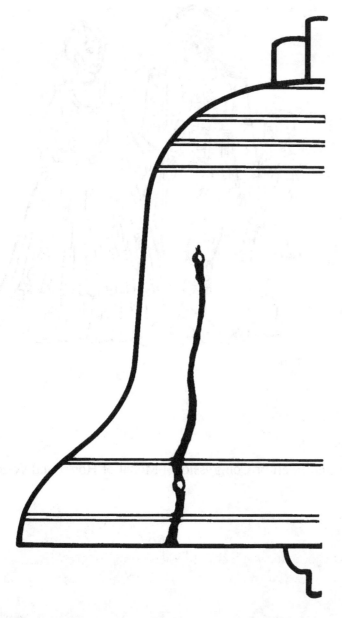

Exploring Biography and Autobiography: Courageous Men of the Revolution

The heroes of the Revolutionary War have earned a special place in the hearts of Americans. These men fought six long, bloody years against the British, the mightiest military force of their time. The biography and autobiography section of a library or learning center contains a wealth of information about these courageous people under the call number "92." (Remember, a biography is a written account of a person's life by someone else; an autobiography is a written account of a person's life story by him/herself). Let's go on a literary journey to learn more about these people who shaped our nation.

Complete the following activities to learn more about these Revolutionary War heroes.

Activity A: Go to your library or learning center and browse through the biography and autobiography section. Take your time in selecting a book about a Revolutionary War hero. Here are just a few suggestions:

- Artemus Ward
- Henry Knox
- Esek Hopkins
- John Hancock
- Nathaniel Green

- Casimir Pulaski
- John Wilke
- John Paul Jones
- John Glover
- Baron Friedrich Wilhelm von Steuben

After reading the selected book, write a brief summary highlighting the major events in this person's life. Explain how this person's courage contributed to the cause of American independence.

Activity B: Share your findings with your classmates by assuming the identity of the person about who you read and telling your life story. You may wish to dress up as this individual or use props to assist you in bringing this person to life.

Courage: Those Who Dared to Make a Difference

Culminating Activities

Word Search: Courageous People

Directions: Find the names of the courageous people listed below in the word search. Names appear horizontally (forwards and backwards), vertically (up and down), and diagonally (corner to corner).

```
S H E P A R D L N Z L I N C O L N D A
H B O C O N N O R E V E R E L M J F T
Q E P S O E A N K S E N O N E A K L D
W C N E R L T M A I D K B A L B O A E
A K N R E S U N B D I C L H E B F G I
S H E R Y A R M S T R O N G T O C I A
H O L L J K Z Z B X E R P N R T D E S
I L G Y L N O S D U H T R I N T S N E
N L E N D E S A L D S E C K A K L A R
G E D C P K R S L I U Z Z O E O N L E
T W I R R E P R E N O S R A C E O L T
O K G A R N C O U S T E A U M V D E R
N C P D K P H R V P M O I T H E S G E
O A K A S B E S L A E L N I R D L A H
Z L I M N O G H S I B U T C H E R M T
F B T S A H N O S N I B O R U R A O O
R E W O H N E S I E A R S M O H E N M
M A D E G S C H I N D L E R C E S Y N
H U D S O N N K K E L L E R I N A H M
```

1. Abbott
2. Adams
3. Aldrin
4. Armstrong
5. Balboa
6. Blackwell
7. Butcher
8. Carson
9. Columbus
10. Cortez
11. Cousteau
12. Eisenhower
13. Glenn
14. Hudson
15. Keller
16. King
17. Lincoln
18. Liuzzo
19. Magellan
20. Mother Teresa
21. O'Connor
22. Paine
23. Parks
24. Ride
25. Revere
26. Robinson
27. Schindler
28. Shepard
29. Washington

#620 Courage　　　186　　　© Teacher Created Materials, Inc.

The Many Faces of Courage

Certain characters from all the novels you read have something important in common—they possess courage. However, they may also have shared other important qualities. Below is a chart listing some important values. Choose four characters from four different novels. Then fill in the chart, giving specific examples of the characters' actions that reflect each of these values. Write "none" if you are unable to think of anything.

Characters

Values				
Willingness to Make Personal Sacrifices				
A Sense of Justice or Fairness				
Perseverance				
Honesty				
Independent Thinking				

Creating a Portrait Gallery

Imagine that you and your classmates are designing your own portrait gallery of courageous people. Choose someone you would like to include in this gallery—a real person, not a fictional character. It might even be someone you know personally. Your task is to draw or find a picture of the courageous person whom you choose. Then draw or place his or her picture in the frame below. Cut out the frame and decorate it. (Another option would be to design your own picture frame made of any material of your choice.) Then write a caption in a few sentences explaining why you have chosen this person. As a class, discuss how and where you will display your pictures and captions to create the portrait gallery.

188

Courage: Those Who Dared to Make a Difference

My Journal

Bibliography

Anderson, Dale. *Explorers Who Found New Worlds.* Austin, Texas: Raintree Steck-Vaughn Publishers, 1994.

Bachrach, Susan D. *Tell Them We Remember.* Boston: Little, Brown, & Co., 1994.

Bailey, Jill and Catherine Thompson, eds. *Planet Earth.* Oxford, England: Oxford University Press, 1993.

Becklake, John. *Man and the Moon.* Morristown, New Jersey: Silver Burdett Co., 1981.

Billington, Elizabeth T. *Understanding Ecology.* New York: Fredrick Warne and Co. Inc., 1968.

Bullard, Sara. *Free at Last: A History of the Civil Rights Movement and Those Who Died in the Struggle.* Montgomery, Alabama: Teaching Tolerance, A Project of the Southern Poverty Law Center, 1989.

Carson, Rachel. *Silent Spring.* Boston: Houghton Mifflin, 1962.

Celsi, Teresa. *Rosa Parks and the Montgomery Bus Boycott.* Brookfield, Connecticut: The Millbrook Press, 1991.

Collier, James Lincoln, and Christopher Collier. *My Brother Sam Is Dead.* Santa Barbara, California: Cornerstone Books, 1974.

Crisman, Ruth. *Racing the Iditarod Trail.* New York: Dillon Press, 1993.

Davis, Burke. *Heroes of the American Revolution.* New York: Random House, 1971.

Dolan, Ellen M. *Susan Butcher and the Iditarod Trail.* New York: Walker Publishing Company, 1993.

Dunbar, Robert E. *How to Debate.* New York: Franklin Watts, 1994.

Frank, Anne. *Anne Frank: The Diary of a Young Girl.* Garden City, New York: Doubleday, 1967.

Friese, Kai. *Rosa Parks: The Movement Organizes.* Englewood Cliffs, New Jersey: Silver Burdett Press, 1990.

Gilford, Henry. *Disastrous Earthquakes.* New York: Franklin Watts, 1981.

Greene, Carol. *Sandra Day O'Connor: First Woman on the Supreme Court.* Chicago: Children's Press, 1982.

Haskins, Jim. *I Have a Dream: The Life and Words of Martin Luther King, Jr.* Brookfield, Connecticut: The Millbrook Press, 1992.

Henrickson, John. *Rachel Carson: The Environmental Movement.* Brookfield, Connecticut: New Directions, The Millbrook Press, 1991.

Bibliography *(cont.)*

Ickis, Marguerite. *The Book of Patriotic Holidays.* Dodd, Mead, and Company, 1962.

Jakoubek, Robert. *Martin Luther King, Jr.* New York: Chelsea House Publishers, 1989.

Kent, Deborah. *The American Revolution, "Give Me Liberty or Give Me Death."* Hillside, New York: Enslow Publishers, Inc., 1994.

Krensky, Stephen. *Four Against the Odds: The Struggle to Save Our Environment.* New York: Scholastic, Inc., 1992.

Lambert, David. *Our World Seas and Oceans.* Morristown, New Jersey: Silver Burdett Press, 1987.

Latham, Jean Lee. *Rachel Carson: Who Loved the Sea.* New York: Chelsea Juniors, 1991.

Liungman, Carl G. *Dictionary of Symbols.* Santa Barbara, California: ABC-CLIO, Inc., 1991.

Lowe, David. *KKK: The Invisible Empire.* New York: W. W. Norton & Company, 1967.

Lowry, Lois. *Number the Stars.* New York: Dell, 1990.

Mallinson, George, et. al. eds. *Science.* Morristown, New Jersey: Silver Burdett and Ginn, 1989.

Mason, Antony. *The Children's Atlas of Exploration.* Brookfield, Connecticut: The Millbrook Press, 1993.

Meltzer, Milton. *Rescue: The Story of How Gentiles Saved Jews in the Holocaust.* New York: Harper & Row Publishers, Inc., 1988.

Meriwether, Louise. *Don't Ride the Bus on Monday: The Rosa Parks Story.* Englewood Cliffs, New Jersey: Prentice-Hall, 1973.

Miller, Marilyn. *The Bridge at Selma.* Morristown, New Jersey: Silver Burdett Press, 1985.

Morris, Richard B. *The American Revolution.* American History Topic Books. Minneapolis: Lerner Publications Company, 1985.

Nardo, Don. *Recycling.* San Diego: Lucent Books Inc., 1992.

New Grolier Multimedia Encyclopedia Release 6. Danbury, Connecticut: Grolier Electronic Publishing, Sherman Turnpike, 1993.

O'Dell, Scott. *Island of the Blue Dolphins.* New York: Dell, 1960.

Parks, Rosa with Gregory J. Reed. *Quiet Strength.* Grand Rapids, Michigan: Zondervan House, 1994.

Parks, Rosa with Jim Haskins. *Rosa Parks: My Story.* New York: Dial Books, 1992.

Bibliography (cont.)

Patrick, Diane. *Martin Luther King, Jr.* New York: Franklin Watts, 1990.

Paulsen, Gary. *Hatchet.* New York: Penguin Books, 1987.

Perkins, Otho E. and Robert L. Stanger. *Work-a-Text in Earth Science.* New York: Globe Book Company, Inc., 1981.

Petrow, Richard. *The Bitter Years.* New York: William Morrow & Co., Inc., 1974.

Polking, Kirk. *Oceans of the World: Essential Resource.* New York: Philomel Books, 1983.

Reef, Catherine. *Rachel Carson: The Wonder of Nature.* Frederick, Maryland: Twenty-First Century Books, 1992.

Resnick, Abraham. *The Holocaust.* San Diego: Lucent Books, Inc., 1991.

Scheller, William. *The World's Greatest Explorers.* Minneapolis: The Oliver Press, Inc., 1992.

Seeger, Pete and Bob Reiser. *Everybody Says Freedom.* New York: W. W. Norton & Company, 1989.

Siegel, Beatrice. *Murder on the Highway: The Viola Liuzzo Story.* New York: Four Winds Press, 1993.

Silverman, Jerry. *Songs of Protest and Civil Rights.* New York: Chelsea House Publishers, 1992.

Stein, Carol R. *The Story of Arlington National Cemetery (Cornerstones of Freedom).* Chicago: Children's Press, 1979.

Taylor, Mildred D. *Roll of Thunder, Hear My Cry.* New York: Penguin Books, 1976.

Tucker, Richard K. *The Dragon and the Cross: The Rise and Fall of the Ku Klux Klan in Middle America.* Hamden, Connecticut: Archon Book, 1991.

Wadsworth, Ginger. *Susan Butcher: Sled Dog Racer.* Minneapolis: Lerner Publications Co., 1994.

"We Are Witnesses." *Newsweek,* April 26, 1993, pages 48-51.

World Atlas for Multimedia IBM PC and Compatible Version 4. Novato, California: The Software Tool Works, 1993.

Wright, David K. *The Story of the Vietnam Memorial (Cornerstones of Freedom).* Chicago: Children's Press, 1989.

Wright, Thomas. *The Undersea World.* Morristown, New Jersey: Silver Burdett Press, 1981.

"Yes and No to the Holocaust Museums." *Commentary,* Volume 96, #2, August, 1993, pages 23–32.

Wojciechowska, Maia. *Shadow of a Bull.* New York: Atheneum, 1970.

Zinsser, William. *Smithsonian,* September, 1991, pages 32-43.

Answer Key *(cont.)*

Number the Stars: Questions from the Novel

Chapters 1-4 (p. 15)

1. When a foreign army resides in another country and rules that country, the country is "occupied." On their way home from school, Annemarie, Kirsti, and Annemarie's friend Ellen are stopped and questioned by Nazi soldiers. There are Nazi soldiers on almost every street corner in Copenhagen. The Johansens, as well as other citizens of Denmark, are unable to buy coffee, tea, butter, or sugar. They have no fuel to heat their homes. Electricity is rationed, so they burn candles at night. They have no rubber for tires. Food is scarce, so the Johansens often eat potatoes for dinner. There is no leather available for shoes. The Nazis order the closing of Jewish shops. Shortly afterward, the Nazis raid the homes of Danish Jews and imprison them.

2. "Resist" means "to fight against." The Danish Resistance is a group of Danish citizens who secretly oppose the Nazis. Their purpose is to sabotage the Nazi Army in any way possible. The Danish Resistance is responsible for bombings in Hillerod and Norrebro. The Resistance also publishes an underground newspaper. It tells of bombs that have exploded in factories that make war goods and bombs that have damaged railroad lines. Members of the Resistance also sabotage German cars and trucks.

3. The people of Denmark love King Christian X. Every morning the king rides on horseback through the streets of Copenhagen to greet his people. One morning, Mr. Johansen overhears a German soldier ask a teenage boy who the man who rides horseback every morning is. The boy replies that the man is the King of Denmark. The soldier then asks, "Where is his bodyguard?" The boy responds with the words, "All of Denmark is his bodyguard."

4. Peter Neilsen informs the Johansens about the latest news regarding the Nazis. Peter says that the Nazis have closed many Jewish stores. Peter warns Annemarie to watch over Ellen and to keep away from the Nazi soldiers. It is dangerous for Peter to visit the Johansens because the Nazis have imposed an eight o'clock curfew on Danish citizens.

5. The fireworks Kirsti refers to were not in celebration of her birthday, as Mama had told her. Instead, these explosions in the night sky are caused by the Danes destroying their own naval fleet. The Danes prefer to destroy these vessels rather than let the Germans gain control of them.

6. Ellen is staying with the Johansens because the Germans plan to raid the homes of Danish Jews and "relocate" them. Mr. and Mrs. Johansen hide Ellen by pretending that she is their daughter, Lise. Peter Neilsen has found a safe place for Ellen's parents to hide. The Johansen apartment is small. It is not possible for the Johansens to hide Mr. and Mrs. Rosen without arousing the Nazis' suspicion.

7. The rabbi of the Rosens' synagogue warns his congregation that the Nazis have the names and addresses of the Jewish congregants. The rabbi also tells his congregation that the Nazis plan to arrest and imprison the Jews.

Answer Key (cont.)

Chapters 5-8 (p. 16)

1. Annemarie knows that on a rainy evening three years ago, Lise was out with her fiance, Peter Neilsen. Lise was hit by a car and died; her death occurred two weeks before her wedding. Annemarie does not know the details of the accident.

2. The Nazi soldiers knock on the Johansen's door in the middle of the night. The soldiers are looking for the Rosens. The Nazis suspect that the Johansens are hiding the Rosens, who are not in their own apartment when the Nazis conduct their search. The soldiers are angry. They speak harshly to the Johansens. One soldier grabs a handful of Ellen's dark hair and suspects that she is Jewish. When Mr. Johansen hands the soldier separate pictures of his three daughters at birth, the soldier drops the pictures on the floor and grinds the heels of his boots into them before he leaves the apartment.

3. Annemarie sees that the Nazi soldiers are in her living room and kitchen. Before the soldiers enter her bedroom, Annemarie quickly tells Ellen to take off her necklace which would identify her as a Jew. Because Ellen cannot unhook the clasp, Annemarie breaks it and hides the necklace in her clenched hand.

4. The Johansens are blonde, like many other Scandinavian people. Jewish people typically have dark hair. Since Ellen's hair is dark, the soldiers suspect she is Jewish. Mr. Johansen convinces the soldiers that Ellen is his daughter, Lise. He shows the soldiers a photograph of Lise as an infant because Lise had dark, curly hair as a baby.

5. Mr. Johansen fears that the Nazi soldiers might search the schools looking for Jewish children. Mrs. Johansen will take Annemarie, Kirsti, and Ellen to her brother Henrik's house in the country near the sea. Mrs. Johansen tells her husband that it will look suspicious if their entire family leaves the apartment and that it would be better for Mr. Johansen to go to his office as usual.

6. Mr. Johansen asks Henrik if the weather is good for fishing. Mr. Johansen says that his wife is coming to visit today with the children and that Mrs. Johansen will bring one carton of cigarettes. Mr. Johansen says that there are many more cartons of cigarettes in Copenhagen now. He tells Henrik that offers will come to him also. Mr. Johansen speaks in code, and he is telling Henrik that Mrs. Johansen and their daughters are bringing a Jewish person to Henrik's house. When Mr. Johansen speaks of "other cartons of cigarettes," he means there are other Jews trying to escape from the Nazis.

7. The German soldier hopes to trap Mrs. Johansen with his question. He wants to learn whether or not she is a Jew since it is the time of the Jewish New Year.

8. Annemarie is afraid Kirsti will tell the soldiers that Ellen is Jewish and it is Ellen's New Year. Answers will vary as to whether or not Mr. and Mrs. Johansen should have told Kirsti about the plan. Most students will probably agree that it is safer for Kirsti not to know.

9. Annemarie tells Ellen that she has hidden her necklace in a secret place. Annemarie plans to keep it hidden until Ellen can safely wear it again.

10. Annemarie has never heard her parents mention Great-Aunt Birte nor has she ever seen a picture of her. No one phoned them in Copenhagen to inform her family of Great-Aunt Birte's death, and no one appears to be mourning.

Chapters 9-12 (p. 17)

1. Annemarie decides that it is safer for Ellen to believe that Great-Aunt Birte is in the casket. Just as Annemarie's mother and uncle try to protect Annemarie, Annemarie protects her friend Ellen. Annemarie realizes that it is easier to be brave if you do not know too much.

2. Mama tells Annemarie that the mourners are friends of Great-Aunt Birte. However, they are in reality other Jews who are trying to escape the Nazis. The mourners at Great-Aunt Birte's wake do not seem to know each other. They do not speak to each other. In contrast, the mourners at Lise's wake brought food and spoke quietly about their memories of Lise.

3. "Staccato" means "brief" or "abrupt." The Nazi soldiers pound on the door of Henrik's house because they are suspicious of the large gathering of people at Henrik's house. The soldiers walk across the floor with short, abrupt clicks of their boots. "Recur" means "to occur or happen again." This scene evokes the same terror in Annemarie as she experienced the night the Nazis raided the Johansen's house when they looked for the Rosens.

4. The Nazis want to know why the casket is closed; it is the custom of the Danish people to view the body of their deceased loved ones at a wake.

5. Typhus is a serious disease carried by lice and fleas. Its symptoms include high fever, weakness, headache, and a dark red rash. Mrs. Johansen thinks quickly and responds to the soldiers' skepticism by saying that Great-aunt Birte died of typhus, which, according to their country doctor, may still be contagious in an open casket. Then, Mrs. Johansen offers to open the casket.

6. Peter will lead a small group of Jewish people gathered at Henrik's home to the harbor where Henrik's boat is docked. Peter also has a secret packet that must be delivered to Henrik.

7. The casket holds an assortment of warm clothes and blankets. The Jewish people will need to wear warm clothing since they plan to escape to Sweden by boat, and it will be cold on the sea.

8. Peter gives the baby, Rachel, a sleeping potion. The Jews will be hiding on Henrik's boat. If the Nazis search the boat and the baby cries out, everyone's life will be in danger. Answers will vary, but most students will probably conclude that Peter's action is necessary.

9. Peter asks Mr. Rosen to give a packet to Henrik. Mr. Rosen does not know what the packet contains, and Peter does not tell him.

10. Peter instructs Mrs. Johansen to wait twenty minutes after he leaves with the first group of Jewish people. Then Mrs. Johansen is to take the Rosens to Henrik's boat. Peter warns her to take the back path and to remain in the shadows to avoid being detected.

11. Peter is now an adult and an equal of Mrs. Johansen. Peter calls her by her first name, Inge. Peter is confident and instructs the group about his plan. Peter is serious and purposeful. He is no longer the lighthearted young man once engaged to Lise.

12. It is about 4:00 A.M. when Annemarie awakens. The early light of dawn is just appearing in the sky. Annemarie expects her mother at 3:30 A.M., but Mrs. Johansen has not yet returned home from the harbor.

Answer Key *(cont.)*

Chapters 13-15 (p. 18)

1. About halfway home from the harbor, Mrs. Johansen stumbles and injures her ankle, probably breaking it. She crawls along the path toward Henrik's home, and that is why it has taken her so long to return.

2. It is Henrik's usual routine to leave at dawn each day to go fishing. If he leaves any earlier, the Nazis might suspect his actions.

3. Annemarie offers to take the packet to her Uncle Henrik. Since Mrs. Johansen's ankle is injured, Annemarie is the only one who can deliver the packet before Henrik's boat departs. Mrs. Johansen instructs Annemarie to place the packet at the bottom of a small basket and to cover it with bread. Mrs. Johansen warns her daughter that she might be stopped by the Nazis. She is to pretend that she is just a silly girl taking her uncle his lunch, which he has forgotten.

4. Annemarie wants to avoid any soldiers who might be on the road to the harbor. They will be looking for Jewish escapees. Annemarie decides that it is safer to remain on the path through the woods.

5. Answers will vary. Students may assume that Annemarie recalls the story to take her mind off the dangerous errand she is undertaking. The story is also familiar to Annemarie because she often told it to her younger sister. Also, Annemarie is probably aware of the similarity between Little Red Riding Hood and herself as they both carry a basket of food and face danger in the woods.

6. Four Nazi soldiers with two large dogs stop Annemarie and question her. They search her basket and throw the bread to the dogs.

7. Annemarie tells the soldiers that she is taking her uncle his lunch, which he has forgotten.

8. She thinks of how Kirsti reacted when the soldiers in Copenhagen stopped and questioned her on the way home from school. Annemarie decides to chatter as Kirsti did when the soldiers stopped them in Copenhagen. Annemarie tells the soldiers that her uncle doesn't like fish for lunch, especially not raw. Then she chatters about how her mother cooks fish. When one soldier grabs the bread from her basket and pulls it apart, Annemarie angrily tells him not to. Annemarie asks the soldiers what they are doing in the woods. She tells them that they are making her late and ruining her uncle's lunch. She does this so that the soldiers will not suspect her true purpose. Her plan works. The soldiers toss the handkerchief and apple to the ground and tell her to take what's left of the lunch to her uncle.

9. Answers will vary. Most students will probably agree that it is easier for Annemarie to be brave because she doesn't know what is in the packet. Other students might think it is hard to be brave whether she knows what is in the packet or not.

10. Annemarie gives the basket to Henrik. She tells him that Mama sent him his lunch, but the soldiers took Henrik's bread. Henrik thanks Annemarie. He sounds relieved when he sees the open packet. Although Annemarie sees no sign of the Rosens or the others, Henrik assures her that "everything is all right."

Answer Key *(cont.)*

Chapters 16-17 and Afterword (p. 19)

1. Mrs. Johansen tells Kirsti that Ellen's parents came to get Ellen last night.

2. Henrik informs Annemarie that he and Peter smuggle Jews out of Denmark. Henrik and other fishermen have built secret compartments in their boats to hide a few people. Henrik also tells Annemarie that Peter is a member of the Resistance fighters.

3. The Germans are angry that the Danish Jews are escaping. The Germans use trained dogs to sniff out the hidden Jews aboard fishing vessels.

4. The handkerchief contains something that attracts the dogs, plus a drug that temporarily interferes with the dogs' senses of smell. The dogs are then unable to detect the scent of the people hidden aboard the boats.

5. When the Germans begin using dogs to locate the hidden passengers aboard the boats, Peter informs some scientists and doctors in the Resistance of this problem. The scientists develop the drug to temporarily interfere with the dogs' senses of smell. Peter has arranged for the captain of each boat to have a handkerchief treated with this special drug.

6. Two years later, church bells ring throughout Copenhagen to celebrate the end of the war. The Danish flag is flown and people sing the Danish national anthem and dance in the streets. During the war, the Danes had taken care of the homes abandoned by their Jewish friends and neighbors. They watered their plants, dusted their furniture, and polished their candlesticks. In each abandoned apartment, the Danes hang a symbol of freedom from the windows.

7. Peter Neilsen is shot and killed by the Nazis in a public square in Copenhagen as punishment for his work in the Resistance. Before his death, he writes to the Johansens saying that he does not fear death and that he is proud to have helped his country and the Jewish people. He requests that he be buried next to Lise, but the Nazis refuse to return his body after his execution. Peter is buried where he was executed in a grave marked only with a number. Answers will vary as to how students feel; most will feel sad that Peter dies trying to help save the lives of others.

8. Lise was also a member of the Resistance. One evening, the Nazis raided the cellar where Peter, Lise, and others met to plan Resistance activities. During the raid, members of the Resistance tried to escape; some were shot, including Peter, who was wounded in the arm. Lise ran away, too, and a Nazi car ran her over in the streets of Copenhagen and killed her.

9. Annemarie hid Ellen's necklace in a yellow dress that Lise wore on the night she and Peter celebrated their engagement. The necklace was tucked into a pocket of Lise's yellow dress. The dress was kept in a blue trunk which held Lise's wedding dress and other items. Annemarie asks her father to fix the broken clasp on Ellen's necklace. Annemarie plans to wear Ellen's Star of David necklace until her friend returns.

Answer Key

Chapters 16, 17, & Afterword (p. 19) *(cont.)*

10. **Fiction:** The characters in the story are fictional, but they are based on the lives of real people and events that occurred in Denmark during World War II.

    Nonfiction: The Danes truly loved King Christian X; Denmark surrendered to Germany in 1940 and was occupied by the German Army for the next five years; Denmark surrendered to Germany because the German Army was too massive and powerful for the Danes to defeat; King Christian rode on horseback through the streets of Copenhagen each morning to greet his people; the story of the German soldier asking a teenage boy, "Who is that man?" referring to the king, is part of recorded Danish history; the Danes sank their own navy to prevent the Germans from gaining control of their ships; on the eve of the Jewish New Year of 1943, the rabbi in Copenhagen warned his congregation that the Nazis were planning to capture the Jews and "relocate" them; George Duckwitz was a German official who notified the Danish government about the Nazis plan to raid Jewish homes. The Danish officials then revealed the Nazi plan to the leaders in the Jewish community in Copenhagen; the Danes hid their Jewish friends and neighbors (almost all of the Jews living in Denmark) and helped them reach the safety of Sweden; scientists actually developed powder made of dried rabbit's blood and cocaine to attract the Nazi dogs and temporarily destroy their sense of smell; the Danish Resistance actively plotted to sabotage the Nazis in any way that they could. Peter Neilsen's character was based on a real Danish Resistance leader, a young man named Kim Malthe-Braun.

Numbers the Stars: **Thinking About the Novel (p. 20)**

1. The people gathered at the wake of Great-Aunt Birte were Jews fleeing the Nazis. They were about to board Henrik's boat to travel a short distance across the sea to Sweden, where they would be safe.

2. The Danish Jews are like the "scattered sons of Israel" because they must flee their homes in order to escape the Nazis. Resistance fighters like Peter and Henrik help save the lives of these Danish Jews. They aid those who are "broken in spirit," protect them, and help them reach the safety of Sweden. Although this Bible passage refers to a promise long ago that God made to Abraham, it also seems to fit the rescue scene in the novel where the Danes help the Jews escape to Sweden.

3. Annemarie feels like crying, yet she tries hard to be brave. She may be feeling overwhelmed by events happening around her. She cannot imagine how anyone could "number," or count, the stars in the sky. There are too many stars to count, and the sky is so vast. The sky, the ocean, and, in fact, the whole world seems too big, cold, and cruel to her right now, much like the soldiers of the German Army must appear to a young girl.

4. Answers will vary as to how students interpret the title of the novel. They will probably associate numbering the stars with numbering the Jewish lives that were saved by the courage and compassion of the Danish people.

Answer Key *(cont.)*

Teacher Information - Rosa Parks and The Montgomery Bus Boycott (p. 127)

1. Segregation means having separate facilities for Blacks and Whites. Restaurants, schools, drinking fountains, restrooms, and bus stops were just some of the facilities in the South that were segregated.

2. The bus driver ordered Rosa Parks to give up her seat to a White man who boarded the bus after all the seats in the White section had been taken. Parks refused. Parks was expected to comply because of the segregation laws in the South. Seats on the buses were divided into the White section at the front of the bus and the "colored" section in the rear of the bus. The bus driver called the police and had Parks arrested for breaking the law. Answers will vary as to how students feel about this incident.

3. The NAACP stands for the National Association for the Advancement of Colored People. The NAACP works to ensure that African Americans are not deprived of their rights as citizens of the United States.

4. E. D. Nixon was the president of the Alabama branch of the NAACP, and Rosa Parks was the secretary of this organization.

5. After Rosa Parks was arrested, she phoned her mother who then contacted E. D. Nixon. Nixon asked Parks to protest the injustice of having to pay a fine for refusing to give up her seat on the bus, a seat that she, like every other person on the bus, had paid for. Parks agreed, and Nixon, along with others in Montgomery, Alabama, organized a boycott of the bus company. Parks agreed to be a test case to challenge the segregation laws in the South because she was tired of being treated like a second class citizen. Her rights as a citizen of the U.S. were being violated.

6. Most African Americans refused to ride the buses.

7. The homes of Martin Luther King, E. D. Nixon, and other Black leaders were bombed, as were three Black churches. Rosa Parks received phone calls threatening her life.

   In February of 1956 during the boycott, White lawyers unearthed an old law prohibiting boycotts. Rosa Parks, Dr. King, and other ministers (a total of 89 people) were arrested for boycotting the buses without "a just cause or legal excuse."

   Answers will vary. Students may feel angry at the injustices Black people experienced on a daily basis in the South.

8. Black people walked to work, formed car pools, and rode horses or mules. Some took cabs. The Black-owned cab companies in Montgomery stopped at the bus stops and charged the same amount as bus fare—ten cents. Churches collected money and purchased their own cars for transporting people during the boycott. Some White people transported their Black employees to and from work even though they were threatened for doing so.

   The boycott lasted for 13 months. It ended on December 20, 1956, when the Supreme Court in a written order said that Montgomery's segregation laws were unconstitutional. The very next day in Montgomery, Black people began riding the buses again.

Roll of Thunder, Hear My Cry: Questions from the Novel

Chapter 1 (p. 105)

1. During the Reconstruction period after the Civil War, the Grangers sold their land to a Yankee for tax money. Grandpa Logan bought two hundred acres of this land in 1887 when it was for sale. Then, in 1918 after he had paid off his mortgage on the land, Grandpa Logan bought another two hundred acres.

2. Papa needs the money to pay the mortgage on two hundred acres of the land and to pay the taxes on the entire four hundred acres.

Answer Key *(cont.)*

Chapter 1 (cont.)

3. The Logans own their land while most other families that they know are sharecroppers on the Granger plantation.

4. T.J. Avery was fourteen years old, tall, and thin. He is in Mrs. Logan's seventh grade class again this year. He is dishonest. He lies to his mother about why he went to the Wallace store. Claude is punished for T.J.'s lie. Mrs. Avery gave Claude a beating, and T.J. laughs about it. Claude is T.J.'s younger brother. Claude is afraid of T.J., so he does not tell his mother the truth.

5. T.J. tells the Logan children that Mr. Berry and his two nephews are seriously burned by some White men.

6. The bus carries White children from the Jefferson Davis County School. The driver does not slow down for Black children as they walk along the dirt road to their school. Stacey and the others climb the bank at the side of the road to avoid being enveloped in a cloud of red dust as the bus passes them. Little Man does not climb up the bank as Stacey had directed. When the bus sped by, the White children laughed as Little Man is covered with dust. Little Man is angry and confused by this incident. He wants to know where his school bus is. The incident illustrates the prejudice and cruelty that Black children experienced everyday. It also illustrates that White children rode buses to school while Black children walked for miles.

7. The facilities for the Whites are better than those for Blacks. The White Jefferson Davis County School has one long White wooden building and a sport field with benches. White children have two buses to take them to school. Also, the White children attend school from the end of August until June.

   The Black children have to walk miles to the Great Faith Elementary and Secondary School. It is a dismal school made up of "four weather-beaten wooden houses on stilts of bricks." The school year for Black children is shortened from October until March because Black children are needed to plant and harvest crops on the plantations. The school for Blacks also lacks current books, desks, paper, blackboards, erasers, maps, and chalk.

8. Little Man can read. He notices the inside cover of the book and finds it was first used by White children for ten years. When the pages were old and worn, then it was given to the Negro children. He could almost accept the book's poor condition, but he could not accept the injustice of being given a book discarded by Whites.

9. Mama quietly listens to Miss Crocker as she explains what happened. Then Mama asks if Miss Crocker punished them. When Miss Crocker says she did, Mama quietly thanks her, but refuses to take Miss Crocker's side. Instead, Mama opens the front cover of the books that Cassie and Little Man refused to take. She understands why they did this. Mama then takes glue and paper and covers the offensive pages for Cassie and Little Man. She also does so for her seventh grade students, so they need not feel inferior to the White children. It seems unlikely that Mama will punish Cassie and Little Man because she understands their anger about the discrimination they have felt.

10. Instead of being grateful for the books, Mama realizes the injustice of the situation. She does not feel that she or other Black people have to accept the way things are.

Answer Key (cont.)

Chapters 2-3 (p. 106)

1. Mr. Morrison is a muscular Black man who towers above Papa's 6'2" height. Mr. Morrison's face is partially scarred, as if he were burned in a fire, and his hair is gray. Papa says that Mr. Morrison is staying with them because he lost his job at the railroad and couldn't find any other work. Mama asks Papa if he had received her letter and he nods yes. The letter probably contained information about the burnings. Mr. Morrison is there to protect the Logan family in Papa's absence.

2. At a gas station in Strawberry, the White men accuse John Henry of flirting with a woman named Sallie Ann. John Henry, Henrietta, and Beacon leave the gas station before trouble begins. John Henry and Beacon drop Henrietta off at her house. Later, on the road, the White men catch up to John Henry and begin to ram John Henry's car. John Henry stops at his uncle's house for help. His uncle tries to stop the White men, but they set fire to John Henry, his uncle, and Beacon. John Henry dies from his wounds.

   The law does not equally value the lives of Blacks and Whites. When Henrietta tries to explain to the sheriff what she witnessed at the gas station, the sheriff calls her a liar.

3. Mama and Papa hear that some older children are drinking liquor and smoking cigarettes at the Wallace store. Mama and Papa sense that there will be trouble for Black children at that store.

4. The White bus driver intentionally tries to run the children off the road. When he sees the children, he speeds up, splashes mud on them, and sends them scurrying up the side of the road to safety. The White children on the bus laugh and ridicule the Black children.

5. Stacey, Cassie, Christopher John, and Little Man skip lunch and borrow some garden tools from the shed at school. They walk to the section where the bus driver ran them off the road. There the Logan children dig a ditch and fill it with rain water so no one will notice it. They make it appear as if the rain has washed out the road. After school, the Logan children hurry to that spot to watch the school bus get stuck in the ditch. Answers will vary as to whether or not students think that the Logan children were justified in their revenge.

6. Mr. Avery comes to warn Mrs. Logan that the night riders will be out that night. Mr. Avery wants to know if Mr. Morrison is there at the Logan's house.

7. The children are terrified. They think the night riders are coming to burn them out of their house because they dug the ditch that wrecked the school bus. Stacey feels responsible.

8. Big Ma takes out a rifle from under her bed and sits in a chair by the window to watch for the night riders. Mr. Morrison had a shotgun in has hand as he guards the house from the outside. Mama has gone into the boys' room to protect them.

9. Cassie awakens in the middle of the night and notices that Big Ma is no longer sitting in her chair by the window. Then Cassie hears a noise on the front porch. Thinking it is her brothers, she goes outside to investigate. The Logan's dog, Jason, knocks Cassie into the flower bed. As she climbs back onto the porch, she sees a caravan of cars in the night. Answers will vary as to whether students think Cassie is brave.

10. Perhaps they think it is better not to tell the children because it will frighten them. Student answers will vary as to whether the adults should speak frankly to their children. Students will probably point out that the children can sense that something is wrong.

Answer Key *(cont.)*

Chapter 4 (p. 107–108)

1. T.J. is lazy. He tells Stacey that the best way to avoid work is not to be around when the work needs to be done. T.J. is also dishonest and sneaky. He hints that Stacey should steal the questions for the next big history test from Mrs. Logan. T.J. says he must go back into the Logan's house to get his cap. He sneaks into Mama's room to look for the test questions. T.J. also suggests that he and Stacey sneak down to the Wallace store. Later, T.J. makes a set of cheat notes that Stacey rips up before the history test. T.J. then makes a second set of cheat notes. During the history test, T.J. passes his cheat notes to Stacey because T.J. does not want to get caught cheating. When Stacey is caught with the cheat notes, T.J. unfairly lets Stacey take a whipping as punishment for something that he had done.

2. Mr. Tatum tells Jim Burnett, a store owner in Strawberry, that he did not order certain things. The Logan children think that the night riders are after them for causing the school bus to break down. They are relieved to find out otherwise.

3. Cassie is comforted by Mr. Morrison's presence. She feels safe with him around. Stacey says that he likes Mr. Morrison, yet he acts unfriendly toward him. Stacey feels that since he is the eldest male in the Logan household, he should be able to protect the family and do a man's work in his father's absence.

4. Stacey goes to the Wallace store looking for T.J., who purposely hid there because he did not think Stacey would follow him. Cassie and Little Man follow Stacey to see what Stacey will do to T.J. Christopher-John objects because he does not want to be punished. However, Christopher-John eventually follows them because he does not want to be left behind.

5. Mr. Morrison expects Stacey to tell his mother himself. Stacey probably tells his mother because his conscience is bothering him. He tells her because he knows it is the right thing to do. Stacey takes responsibility for his actions. He accepts the consequences of his behavior.

6. Mr. Granger pressures Big Ma to sell her land when David Logan is away working on the railroad. Although Mr. Granger does not need the land, he is greedy. Also, Harlan Granger is the kind of person to hold a grudge for years. He is still angry with Wade Jamison for selling the second 200 acres of land to the Logans.

7. After the Civil War, the Grangers were financially ruined. Their Confederate money was worthless. During the Civil War the Northern and Southern armies damaged the Granger plantation. The Grangers sold 2,000 acres of their land to rebuild their plantation and to pay their taxes on the land that remained. Later, the Yankee who bought their 2,000 acres offered to sell it back to Harlan Granger's father. His father refused because he did not want to part with his money.

8. Answers will vary. Students may see Big Ma as weak. They might point out that she was afraid of Mr. Anderson's threat so she let Mr. Anderson's lumbermen cut down the forest on her land. David Logan had to return home to stop the destruction of the forest.

9. Mrs. Logan wants her children to see what kind of trouble they could become involved in at the Wallace store. The Wallaces had badly burned Mr. Berry and his two nephews. One of the nephews, John Berry, died due to his injuries. Some students may think it was wise of Mrs. Logan to let her children see for themselves what could happen to them.

10. Mrs. Logan asks the parents of some of her students not to allow their children to go to the Wallace store because of the smoking and drinking permitted there. She also attempts to organize a boycott of the Wallace store by the neighboring sharecroppers. Mrs. Logan organizes the boycott despite the threat of the night riders who terrorize Black people whom they feel are stepping out of line.

Answer Key *(cont.)*

Chapter 4 (cont.)

11. Mrs. Logan is a woman of principles. Even though shopping in Vicksburg is inconvenient because it requires an overnight journey, she shops there anyway because the storekeepers in Vicksburg treat her with respect.

12. Mr. Montier takes half the money Mr. Turner earns from raising cotton. Mr. Montier signs for Mr. Turner's credit at the Wallace store, but Mr. Montier charges Mr. Turner 10-15 percent of Mr. Montier's debt as "risk money."

13. Students will probably think that Mr. Turner is courageous. Although Mr. Turner knows he could be set on fire by "angry White men and night riders," he agrees to boycott the Wallace store and give his business to the Vicksburg storekeepers if someone will back his credit.

Chapter 5 (p. 109)

1. Cassie suggests that they move their wagon closer to the market entrance since they have arrived early and there is still plenty of room. Big Ma says that is where White folks park their wagons.

2. Cassie likes Mr. Jamison even though he is White because he treats the Logan family with respect. He is the only White man that Cassie knows who calls Big Ma "Missus." Cassie also likes Mr. Jamison because, like her father, Mr. Jamison will give a person a straight answer when he is asked a question. Cassie is not prejudiced. She judges Mr. Morrison by how he treats others, not by the color of his skin.

3. T.J. looks longingly at a pearl-handled handgun. He says he needs the gun for protection. T.J. says he wouldn't need anybody if he had that gun. T.J. claims that he would sell his life for that gun, and one day he will have it.

4. Cassie does not understand why T.J. wants the gun. She says it is very expensive and that it is not good for hunting. Stacey politely tells T.J. that it is a nice looking gun. However, the gun does not fascinate Stacey in the same way that it fascinates T.J.

5. Answers will vary. Students might observe that the Logan children are protected by the adults in their family. Cassie thinks about the shotgun her father has and the rifle Big Ma keeps locked in a trunk under her bed. Perhaps that sense of adult protection is missing in T.J.'s family life.

6. Cassie feels it is unfair that Mr. Barnett waits on White people in the middle of filling T.J.'s order. Cassie can almost accept the situation when Mr. Barnett is waiting on adults. However, when he stops to fill the order of a White girl who is no bigger than Cassie, Cassie nicely tells him that she thinks he has forgotten about them. Mr. Barnett yells at Cassie and humiliates her. He bans her from shopping in his store until her mother teaches her "what she is." Answers will vary as to whether students see Cassie's action as courageous or foolish.

7. Stacey means that he cannot change Mr. Barnett. Stacey feels it is better to avoid confronting Mr. Barnett about his behavior because it would not do any good.

8. Cassie accidentally bumps into Lillian Jean on the sidewalk. Lillian Jean demands an apology, and Cassie refuses. Lillian Jean then tries to push Cassie off the sidewalk. Cassie avoids her, but Mr. Simms, Lillian Jean's father, gruffly knocks Cassie onto the road. He also insists that Cassie apologize and address Lillian Jean as "Miz."

9. Jeremy tells Lillian Jean to leave Cassie alone. When Mr. Simms demands that Cassie apologize to Lillian Jean, Jeremy tells his father that Cassie already did. Mr. Simms just glares at his son.

10. Students might feel angry, humiliated, and sad. Answers will vary. Students may point out that Big Ma was powerless in the presence of Mr. Simms and the other White people from Mr. Barnett's store who are watching the incident. Other students may feel that Big Ma is a coward.

Answer Key *(cont.)*

Chapter 6 (p. 110)

1. Hammer might be trying to show that he is equal to any White man, including Harlan Granger.

2. Hammer is enraged by the injustice of the situation. Hammer says if he had pushed Lillian Jean off the sidewalk, he would have been lynched. When Big Ma tells Hammer to "let it be" because Cassie is not hurt, Hammer replies, "Not hurt! You look into her eyes and tell me she ain't hurt!" Hammer has a gun and he angrily drives off in his Packard, probably heading toward Charlie Simms' house.

3. Mr. Morrison probably affirms Hammer's anger, but convinces Hammer that the Logans will be harmed more if Hammer confronts Mr. Simms.

4. Mama explains the story of slavery. She points out that Mr. Simms holds onto the belief that he is better than Black people because he has "little else to hold on to." Mama tells Cassie that they do not give people like the Simms their respect, but they do fear them. This is why Big Ma made Cassie apologize to Lillian Jean.

5. T.J. ridicules Stacey by calling him Reverend Logan. He says that Stacey looks like a preacher in that coat. T.J. is jealous of Stacey's good fortune.

6. Big Ma tells Hammer he would be hanged.

7. Hammer refuses to back off Soldiers Bridge when an old Model-T truck approaches the bridge. The Wallaces are in the truck. They mistake Hammer's car for Harlan Granger's car, so the Wallaces back off the bridge. The Wallaces are surprised to see the Logans in the car when they cross the bridge. Mama says someday the Logans will pay for what Hammer has done.

Chapter 7 (p. 111)

1. T.J. ridiculed Stacey by saying the coat was too big. T.J. persuaded his friends to do the same. Answers will vary. Some students may feel that Hammer was justified because he was trying to teach Stacey a lesson that he should not let others take advantage of him. Other students might feel that Hammer was taking out his anger about other things on Stacey.

2. "Night men" attacked his family for harboring two teenage boys accused of molesting a White woman. The night men burned the home of Mr. Morrison's family and killed his parents and sisters.

3. The Logans organize a boycott of the Wallace store. Papa, Hammer, and Mr. Morrison travel to Vicksburg looking for someone to extend credit to thirty families.

4. On Christmas Day, Jeremy comes to the Logan house to give Stacey a flute that he made. If Jeremy's father had known what he did, Jeremy would be punished.

5. Answers will vary. Students may point out that because of race, society did not view the two boys as equal. This would make a true friendship between them impossible. Other students may disagree. They may feel that as long as Jeremy and Stacey view themselves as equal, a friendship is possible. It does not matter how society views their friendship.

6. Big Ma will no longer be pressured by Harlan Granger to sell her land since David and Hammer would be the legal owners. Also, upon Big Ma's death, Harlan Granger could not claim the land as his own.

7. Mr. Jamison is bothered by the injustice of the Wallaces' actions. Mr. Jamison knows he cannot have the Wallaces put in jail for John Berry's death, but he can hurt the Wallaces financially. Mr. Jamison also knows that if the Logans back the sharecroppers' credit, they will lose their land. Although Mr. Jamison realizes that some people will be angry that he is backing the credit of the sharecroppers, he does it anyway.

8. Harlan Granger owns the land the Wallace store is on, so he gets a percentage of the store's profits.

Answer Key (cont.)

Chapter 7 (p. 111, cont.)

9. The Logans organize the boycott of the Wallace store as an example of justice for their children. They want their children to stand up for justice in the face of danger. Perhaps someday their children's lives will be different.

10. Harlan Granger threatens that the Logans will lose their land if they continue the boycott. He says that since the price of cotton is low, he might have to charge his sharecroppers more next year to meet his own expenses. Then, his sharecroppers will have little money left to buy winter supplies and pay their debts. Harlan Granger also claims that the bank which holds the Logan mortgage on their land will no longer honor their loan.

Chapters 8-9 (p. 112)

1. Cassie calls Lillian Jean "Miz" whenever she sees her. Cassie pretends to accept Lillian Jean's opinion of her as an inferior. She carries Lillian Jean's books to school, and Lillian Jean confides her secrets to Cassie. After a month of doing this, Cassie leads Lillian Jean to a dark section of the forest and beats her. When Lillian Jean threatens to tell her father, Cassie says she will blab Lillian Jean's secrets to everyone at Jefferson Davis County School. Furthermore, Cassie says that Lillian Jean's friends will probably admire Cassie's cleverness and her sense of justice.

2. Harlan Granger, Kaleb Wallace, and another man visit Mama's classroom to hear her teach. Mama is teaching a history lesson about the injustice of slavery. Harlan Granger says that Mama's lesson is not in the textbook approved by the Board of Education. Harlan Granger has Mama fired for this and for altering a page in her students' textbooks. He wants to punish her for organizing the boycott.

3. T.J. complains at the Wallace store that Mary Logan is not a good teacher because she purposely fails him. T.J. also says that Miz Logan damaged the textbooks and that she is the one who is organizing the boycott of the Wallace store. The Wallaces then inform Harlan Granger.

4. Stacey confronts T.J. who denies that he told the Wallaces anything about their mother. All of the Logan children, as well as their friends, shun T.J.

5. Although R. W. and Melvin Simms act friendly toward T.J., behind his back they ridicule him. T.J. has been shunned by his other friends. He wants attention.

6. Answers will vary. Students might disagree because Harlan Granger has decided to take 60% rather than 50% of the profits from the cotton that the sharecroppers grow. Harlan Granger also threatens to force the families involved in the boycott off his land. Furthermore, the Wallaces threaten that the sheriff will put them on the chain gang to work off the debt they owe the Wallaces.

7. Although Papa would like the Averys and the Laniers to continue boycotting the Wallace store, he understands their predicament. He realizes that though it is hard for them to give up, they seem to have no other choice since they do not own the land they farm.

8. The back wheels fall off the Logan wagon on the way home from Vicksburg. Because someone had sabotaged the wagon. While Papa is under the wagon trying to put the wheels back on, three men drive by in a truck. One of them shoots Papa in the head, but the bullet just grazes Papa's temple. Papa's leg gets caught under the wagon. Stacey tries to hold the mule still, but it bolts. The wagon runs over Papa's leg and breaks it.

9. Mr. Morrison flings one of the men to the ground and may have broken the man's back. One of the other Wallace men appears to have a broken arm.

10. The children are afraid that their father might die as a result of his injuries.

Answer Key (cont.)

Chapters 10-11 (pages 113–114)

1. Hammer gives Papa and Mama half of the money needed to pay the June mortgage. Papa fears that if Hammer learns about the Wallaces attacking Papa, Hammer will punish the Wallaces himself. This will only result in further violence and probably Hammer's death, as well.

2. Kaleb Wallace condemns Mr. Morrison for injuring his two brothers. Kaleb refuses to move his truck. Mr. Morrison first looks inside the truck to be sure that Kaleb does not have a gun. Then Mr. Morrison lifts the truck out of his way with his own tremendous strength and drives off. Kaleb is at first speechless, but then he threatens to harm Mr. Morrison one of these nights.

3. Mr. Morrison is not afraid of Kaleb Wallace. Mr. Morrison could probably have killed Kaleb with his bare hands, yet he restrains himself. Mr. Morrison has no gun; his strength and courage come from within. In contrast, Kaleb is a coward who threatens to come after Mr. Morrison in the middle of the night, though he knows that he is no match for Mr. Morrison. Later, Mr. Morrison tells Mama that Kaleb cannot act without a gun and plenty of other people to back him up.

4. The sheriff will not arrest the Wallaces because they are White. If the Logans report the Wallaces to the sheriff, Mr. Morrison would probably be arrested for attacking White men.

5. T.J. comes to the revival with R. W. and Melvin Simms to try to impress Stacey and his other old friends with his new clothes and to try to make them jealous. T.J. is hurt that his old friends rejected him, but he is too insecure to admit it. Outwardly, T.J. flaunts his new clothes and new friends, but his character has not changed. It is hinted that T.J. stole a watch from Moe Turner and a locket from the Laniers.

6. The bank is now requiring that the Logans immediately repay whatever money they have borrowed to purchase their land. Harlan Granger carried out his threat to convince the bank not to honor the Logans' loan any longer.

7. Uncle Hammer gives them the money to repay the bank. Hammer borrows some of it and sells his new car.

8. T.J. is badly beaten by R. W. and Melvin Simms. T.J. asks Stacey to help him get home so Mrs. Avery can tend to his wounds.

9. R. W. and Melvin convince T.J. to break into the Barnetts' store to steal the pearl-handled gun. R. W. and Melvin steal the gun and break into a wall cabinet. Mr. Barnett surprises them. R. W. hits Mr. Barnett over the head with an ax. Mrs. Barnett becomes involved in the struggle. She hits her head on the stove and is knocked unconscious. T.J. wants to go home, but R. W. and Melvin beat T.J., toss him into the back of their truck, and then go to play pool. T.J. escapes and hitches a ride toward home. On the way he stops at the Logans' house because he needs help.

10. Stacey feels responsible for T.J. Stacey is loyal and trustworthy. He is also courageous.

11. R. W. and Melvin Simms, Kaleb Wallace, and several other men drag T.J. from his house, punch him, and are ready to lynch him. These men also drag Mr. and Mrs. Avery from their house and throw the Avery girls out the open windows of the house. These same men slap and kick the Avery children and fling Mrs. Avery against the side of her house when she tries to stop them from hurting her children.

12. On the night of the robbery, R. W. and Melvin wear masks to conceal their identities. However, T.J. does not wear a mask, so only he can be identified. When T.J. suspects a set-up and wants to leave the store without the gun, R. W. and Melvin refuse. After the robbery, R. W. and Melvin go to shoot pool in town. They lie to the other men in their mob and say that they saw T.J. and two other Black boys running from the Barnett store on the night of the robbery.

Answer Key *(cont.)*

Chapter 11 (p. 113–114, cont.)

13. Mr. Jamison confronts the angry mob at the Avery house. He tells them to let him and the sheriff take T.J. into custody. Mr. Jamison says it is for the court to decide if T.J. is guilty or not. The mob threatens Mr. Jamison, who bravely uses his own body to shield T.J.

14. Kaleb Wallace suggests that the mob go down to the Logan's property and hang Mr. Morrison and Papa, as well.

Chapter 12 (p. 115)

1. Answers will vary. One choice is to use his shotgun. Mary cautions her husband against using violence because she knows that David, Mr. Morrison, and perhaps T.J. may be killed in the fight that would ensue. A second choice might be to offer to sell Harlan Granger the Logans' land. This would break David Logans' spirit. He feels he could never give up his land because it gives him independence and is his source of pride. A third choice is to start the fire. It is a good choice because everyone must work together toward the common goal of putting out the fire before it destroys everything in its path.

2. Mary and Big Ma drench burlap sacks in water and use them to smother the fire.

3. The fire is moving away from the Logan house and toward the forest. It might have burned everything in its path from the Logan farm to Strawberry.

4. They direct everyone to help dig a trench. Then they start a backfire by setting fire to the grass from the trench back to the cotton where the fire is burning. The rain also helps to extinguish the fire.

5. The townspeople think that lightning started the fire.

6. When the night men leave the Avery's house with T.J. in the car, Mr. Jamison drives to Harlan Granger's house and blocks the road with his car to stop the angry mob. When Kaleb Wallace attempts to grab Mr. Jamison's car keys, Mr. Jamison throws them in the flower garden.

7. Harlan Granger is motivated by his own self-interest. He stops the lynching only because he needs everyone's combined efforts to extinguish the fire and save his own land.

8. Mr. Jamison does not want David Logan to call attention to himself by going into the town of Strawberry. He does not want anyone to suspect that David Logan started the fire to stop the lynching.

9. Mr. Barnett dies from his injuries. The sheriff and Mr. Jamison take T.J. to jail to await his trial. Answers will vary as to what else might happen to T.J.

10. Cassie does not fully comprehend the extent of the prejudice Black people faced in the South during the Depression. Although she does not understand prejudice, she knows it will not end quickly. This realization saddens Cassie.

Answer Key (cont.)

Shadow of a Bull: Questions from the Novel (p. 169)

1. Manolo's inner voice is telling him that he is a coward. He is afraid to jump off the pile of hay with his friends, afraid to swim, afraid to ride his bicycle, and most of all, afraid to fight a bull.

2. Many people try to direct the course of Manolo's life. The six men of Arcangel who had followed Juan Olivar's bullfighting career want Manolo to become a famous bullfighter like his father. They take Manolo to bullfights when he reaches the age of nine. They try to teach him everything they know about bullfighting. These men do not have Manolo's best interests at heart. They are only interested in carrying on Juan Olivar's legendary career through Manolo. They never even ask Manolo if bullfighting is something he wishes to learn. Even Manolo realizes that "The six men cared much more for the animals than for the men who fought them." Other people try to influence Manolo as well. The townspeople of Arcangel expect Manolo to become a famous bullfighter. Emilio Juarez, a bullfighter, dedicates a brave bull to Manolo during a bullfight. Juarez also tosses his hat to Manolo during the bullfight. The Count de la Casa selects the bull that Manolo would fight as Manolo approaches his twelfth birthday. Miguel Garcia, Jaime and Juan's father, tell Manolo that he is destined to become a great bullfighter. Even Manolo's mother seems resigned to her son's fate. She even expects Manolo to be grateful for the help that the six men have given him. Since none of these people ever ask Manolo what he wants, it is doubtful that they have his best interests in mind.

3. It is Alfonso Castillo, the famous bullfighting critic, who helps Manolo follow his inner voice. At the Count's tienta, Alfonso Castillo asks if anyone has ever asked Manolo if he wishes to fight the bull. Alfonso senses that Manolo does not want to be a bullfighter, and he respects Manolo's free will. He tells Manolo that he has the choice to please himself or to please others. Alfonso advises Manolo to be what he is and to wait if he does not yet know what he is. Alfonso tells Manolo not to let anyone make his decision for him. Ten years before, a bullfighter had challenged Alfonso Castillo to fight a bull. Alfonso was not sure if that was what he wanted to do. On his way to the bullfight, Alfonso was injured in a car accident. He questions whether he allowed the bullfighter to pressure him into doing something that he did not want to do. Alfonso must be able to follow his own inner voice, or he will not be able to allow others to do so.

Page 186

4. Before the Count's tienta, Manolo feels a tight knot in his stomach. He also feels a choking in his throat. After speaking with Alfonso Castillo, Manolo feels that the burden that once weighed him down has now lifted. Manolo says that although he still felt fear, he is no longer paralyzed by that fear.

5. Alfonso Castillo tells Manolo that he knew Manolo's father well. Castillo says that if Juan Olivar were alive today, Manolo would not be at the tienta. Juan Olivar would have understood that Manolo was not a "carbon copy" of his father. Juan Olivar would probably have realized that his son must follow his own dream.

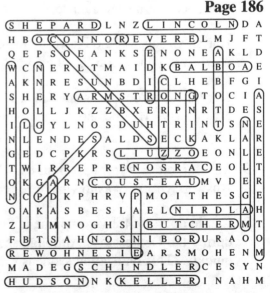